200 gluten-free recipes

200 gluten-free recipes

hamlyn **all color**

An Hachette UK Company
www.hachette.co.uk

First published in Great Britain in 2011 by Hamlyn
a division of Octopus Publishing Group Ltd, Endeavour
House, 189 Shaftesbury Avenue, London, WC2H 8JY
www.octopusbooks.co.uk

Distributed in the USA and Canada by Octopus Books USA:
c/o Hachette Book Group, 237 Park Avenue, New York,
NY 10017

ISBN 13: 978-0-600-62240-6

A CIP catalogue record for this book is available
from the British Library.

Printed and bound in China

10 9 8 7 6 5 4 3

Standard level spoon measurements are used in all recipes.
1 tablespoon = one 15 ml spoon
1 teaspoon = one 5 ml spoon

Ovens should be preheated to the specified temperature – if
using a fan-assisted oven, follow the manufacturer's instructions
for adjusting the time and temperature.

Fresh herbs should be used unless otherwise stated.

Medium eggs should be used unless otherwise stated.

The Food and Drug Administration advises that eggs should
not be consumed raw. This book contains some dishes made
with raw or lightly cooked eggs. It is prudent for vulnerable
people such as pregnant and nursing mothers, invalids, the
elderly, babies, and young children to avoid uncooked or lightly
cooked dishes made with eggs. Once prepared, these dishes
should be kept refrigerated and used promptly.

This book includes dishes made with nuts and nut derivatives. It
is advisable for those with known allergic reactions to nuts and
nut derivatives and those who may be potentially vulnerable to
these allergies to avoid dishes made with nuts and nut oils. It is
also prudent to check the labels of pre-prepared ingredients for
the possible inclusion of nut derivatives.

contents

introduction

introduction

This book aims to show you that cooking for someone with celiac disease need not be difficult or daunting. With careful label checking, combined with the recipes contained here, you will be able to prepare and enjoy a huge range of dishes and goodies—from soups and starters to mains, desserts, and cakes and bakes. Gluten-free alternatives to recipes you wish you could eat are also provided. The meals, snacks, and treats can all be used as part of a meal plan, and you will find something here for all the day's meals whether it's breakfast, lunch, supper, or dessert. With practice, gluten-free cooking will become easier as you get to grips with your repertoire of recipes.

what is gluten?

Gluten is a type of protein found in a number of grains including wheat, barley, and rye. It can also be found in oats if they are processed in the same place as wheat, barley, and rye products and have become cross-contaminated. A few people with celiac disease are also sensitive to pure, uncontaminated oats, although these do not contain gluten. Therefore many people with celiac disease choose to eliminate oats from their diet, too.

Gluten gives elasticity to dough, helping it to rise and to keep its shape, and can give the final product a chewy texture. As grains containing gluten are often the main ingredient in many popular food items, such as breads, cakes, many processed foods, and cereal goods, finding gluten-free alternatives can be challenging. If you experience an oversensitivity to gluten, which often results in unpleasant symptoms, eliminating these products from your diet is a crucial part of food shopping, preparation, and cooking.

what is celiac disease?

Celiac disease is the condition most often associated with an oversensitivity to gluten that causes inflammation in the lining of the small intestine (part of the gut). Celiac disease is not a food allergy or a food intolerance; it is an autoimmune disease whereby the body makes antibodies against the gluten protein.

Antibodies that are usually responsible for attacking bacteria and viruses see the gluten and attack it, in turn causing the inflammation of the lining of the small intestine.

causes, symptoms, and long-term problems

The lining of the small intestine is covered with millions of finger-like projections called villi. When antibodies attack the gluten they cause inflammation, which in turn flattens the villi, meaning that nutrients from food cannot be so readily absorbed. This can result in deficiencies including anemia.

Other symptoms range from mild to severe and can include diarrhea, bloating, abdominal pain, excess wind, and tiredness, or weakness. Often the symptoms of celiac disease are confused with irritable bowel syndrome (IBS) or a wheat intolerance as they manifest themselves similarly. Symptoms can also vary from person to person: in infants celiac presents as a failure to thrive; in children it can cause a lack of appetite, altered bowel habits, and anemia; and within the adult population symptoms include anemia, diarrhea, chronic tiredness, lethargy, weight loss, and other abdominal abnormalities. Other systems of the body could be affected through headaches, hair loss, tooth enamel erosion, and joint pain.

It is important to seek medical advice if you suspect an oversensitivity to gluten, because long-term problems caused by untreated or undiagnosed celiac disease can include:-

- Infertility in women, including recurrent miscarriage
- Poor growth of babies during pregnancy
- Osteoporosis—thinning of bones
- A slightly increased risk of developing bowel cancer, intestinal lymphoma, and cancer of the esophagus.

A gluten-free diet reduces complications as well as other associated conditions such as mouth ulcers and dermatitis herpetiformis. Sticking to a gluten-free diet will see the risk of any cancers associated with celiac disease reduced and brought in line with statistics for the rest of the population.

who suffers from celiac disease?

Almost 1 in 100 people are affected by celiac disease but it is thought that at least 60 percent remain undiagnosed. Anyone, at any age, can develop celiac disease and it is most commonly diagnosed in people aged between 40 and 50. About 1 in 4 cases are first diagnosed in people aged over 60. Celiac disease can be hereditary—if you have a close family member who has celiac disease then you have a 1 in 10 chance of having or developing celiac disease. If you have another autoimmune disease—for example, some thyroid diseases, rheumatoid arthritis and type 1 diabetes—then you are also more predisposed to having or developing celiac disease.

diagnosis and treatment

If you suspect that you have celiac disease, don't remove gluten from your diet immediately. First, consult your doctor, who will carry out a simple blood test to detect if the antibody against gluten is present. If this blood test is positive you may be referred for a biopsy of the lining of the small intestine to see if the tell-tale signs of celiac disease are present. Cutting out gluten before you are tested for celiac disease may give a negative result.

If you test positive then the next step is to completely cut out gluten from your diet for life. Symptoms will usually disappear within a couple of weeks and the small intestine will begin to repair itself. Symptoms will return, however, even if only a tiny amount of gluten is consumed. Your doctor should refer you to a dietitian who can give you advice on how to deal with celiac disease and what you should and shouldn't eat. The internet is another important port of call—there are several foundations, that provide support in the form of ists all gluten-free foods, shopping guides and more. The Celiac Disease Foundation and the National Foundation for Celiac Awareness both provide resources and links to other organizations or suppliers. It is worth trying to keep up-to-date with the latest scientific advice and these organizations' websites both offer helpful advice.

following a gluten-free diet

Bearing in mind that gluten is present in all wheat, barley, and rye products, and very often in oats through cross-contamination, careful thought needs to be given to shopping for, preparing and cooking a gluten-free diet.

Most manufacturers label products that are gluten-free, with some variation of a grain with a cross or bar through it. Even if the packaging doesn't show you the information in a visual way, you will be able, by looking at the list of ingredients, to identify if any products containing gluten are used in processed items.

Some foods that contain gluten are obvious —breads, cakes, pastries, cookies, and pasta, for instance. Others, such as processed foods including some soups, chips, and sausages, may also contain gluten, so a good study of food labels is essential. But don't panic! Take a look round at all the wonderful foods that are naturally gluten-free (see below) and you will see that these can be used to make delicious meals. A quick read through of the recipes in this book will also reveal that gluten-free cooking can still be exciting using some of the substitutes listed in the 'Pantry Essentials' section on page 13.

foods that are naturally gluten-free

- Fruits and vegetables, including potatoes
- Unprocessed meat, poultry and fish
- Unprocessed cheeses, butter, milk and plain milk products
- Eggs
- Tofu
- Cooking oils
- Sugar, baking soda, cream of tartar, yeast
- Plain nuts, seeds and pulses
- Rice and its products, such as rice noodles and rice flour
- Gluten-free grains and their products, such as buckwheat noodles, cornmeal, and cornstarch
- Plain yogurt
- Vinegars
- Fats

- Coffee and tea
- Herbs and spices

*NB: Some naturally gluten-free grains are milled with wheat, barley and rye and may be cross-contaminated

foods that contain gluten
- Wheat, barley and rye and their products, such as pasta, wheat noodles, bulgur wheat and couscous
- Bread, cakes, cookies, breakfast cereals and snacks/confectionery containing wheat, barley and rye flour
- Baking powder
- Foods covered in batter, breadcrumbs or dusted with flour
- All beers, stouts, lagers and ales
- Barley water/concentrates and malted milk drinks
- Some mustard products may contain wheat as a thickener
- Chinese soy sauce, which is traditionally made from fermented wheat
- Stuffing mixes
- Some ready-made seasonings, sauces, soups, gravy granules, and bouillon cubes

gluten-free store-bought alternatives
As well as the basic foodstuffs that are gluten-free, you can also buy pre-prepared food items that use gluten-free ingredients as a substitute for those containing gluten. Looking round on the supermarket shelves you will see an ever-increasing range of gluten-free products, such as breads, cookies, and pasta, and many of these products have come a long way from the bland, poor-quality gluten-free foods of years gone by. Gluten-free products are not quite the same as traditional goods, however, as it is gluten that gives bread its elasticity and cakes their spring. If you try one product and don't like it, don't despair—try another brand or get baking yourself! Try some of the carefully selected recipes in this book that use gluten-free ingredients to replicate as closely as possible foods that contain gluten.

pantry essentials
As mentioned above, there are many naturally gluten-free products such as unprocessed meat and fish, dairy foods, fresh fruit and vegetables, rice, and legumes. However, you will need to prepare other common foods that are not normally gluten-free—such as white

sauce, gravy, cakes, breads, pasta, and noodle dishes—using gluten-free ingredients. If you look out for and stock up on some of the following items you will be able to make all the recipes in this book whenever you wish.

flours

As well as proprietary flour mixes, there are other gluten-free flours that can be used for baking and cooking such as rice gram, chickpea, potato, soy, corn, buckwheat, and millet—if these are not available in your local supermarket they can usually be found in health food stores or can be ordered online. You don't need to buy them all, however— for general all-purpose use, I find rice flour a great all-rounder and cornstarch is good for sauces and thickening in stews, although it is worth experimenting with other flours as well. This book uses rice flour and cornstarch primarily.

xanthan gum

A powder that greatly aids gluten-free baking. Xanthan gum, to some extent, replaces the elastic qualities that gluten-free flours lack. Adding a little to gluten-free flours makes bread less crumbly and gluten-free pastry easier to roll and handle. It's available in some health food stores and in some supermarkets. I have only used xanthan gum in these recipes where it is really needed, opting to use a variety or mix of other flours to get the best results, in breads, scones, cakes and cookies.

gluten-free baking powder

Standard baking powder contains gluten. Gluten-free baking powder is now widely available in the baking aisles of supermarkets. Baking soda and cream of tartar are naturally gluten-free, so if you prefer to make your own gluten-free baking powder simply mix 2 parts baking soda with 1 part cream of tartar and use this for spoon for spoon.

pasta and noodles

Gluten-free pastas are becoming more common, and are marketed as such. Rice noodles are gluten-free, as are the varieties of soba noodles that are made entirely from buckwheat.

grains

Quinoa is a brilliant addition to the diet, providing an excellent source of protein as well as being gluten-free. It is a great substitute for couscous or bulghur wheat for salads and side dishes. Cornmeal is great for baking and for use as an alternative coating to breadcrumbs. As a form of carbohydrate it can also be used in place of pasta with meals.

legumes

Lentils and beans can be used in stews and casseroles, but are also great in salads or as side dishes.

cheese and dairy

Unprocessed cheeses are gluten-free and brilliant to have to hand in the refrigerator; don't overindulge, though, as they are high in fat! Milk and plain, unflavored yogurts are gluten-free, and it is worth looking at the labels of other dairy products to find gluten-free options.

As with all types of cooking, gluten-free cooking can be a case of trial and error as gluten-free products have different baking qualities and properties. Don't give up if you find you don't get instantly good results—you will get acceptable results eventually. As well as satisfying a gluten-free diet, the rest of the family will also be more than happy with the recipes in this book.

cross-contamination

So you have cut out gluten, found your way round the gluten-free products available and have the gluten-free foods list to hand (see page 11) … all should be plain sailing from here. You and others around you must be aware, however, that cross-contamination is easy: by spreading butter that has been contaminated with 'normal' bread crumbs on your gluten-free toast; by using the same toaster for gluten-free and 'normal' bread; or by stirring a gluten-free dish with a spoon that has been stirring gravy made with wheat flour.

Even small amounts of gluten can cause the symptoms of celiac disease to return. Make the following simple but important tips a part of your routine in order to prevent cross-contamination:

in the home

- Store gluten-free flours separately
- Use separate spoons and knives to prepare gluten-free food
- Keep a gluten-free sifter, rolling pin, pastry brush, and cutting board
- Wash everything well and clean surfaces before cooking and eating

eating out

Check the menu of restaurants where you plan to eat and make sure that staff are aware of your condition prior to your visit. Hidden gluten can be in sauces, coatings (for example, bread crumbs), gravy, and bouillon cubes. Many chefs are happy to cook you something off the menu with your advice, or they can advise on the ingredients used, to ensure you make an informed choice.

making mistakes

When you have eaten gluten by mistake, you usually start to have a few symptoms a few hours after eating and the effects can last from a few hours to several days depending on your sensitivity to what you have eaten. You may want to treat the symptoms or prefer to wait until they naturally get better. If you are having diarrhea or are vomiting it is important to keep yourself well hydrated by drinking lots of water. Some people also find that taking medication to treat constipation, diarrhea, or headaches can ease symptoms, so speak to your pharmacist or physician. The most important thing is to get back onto your gluten-free diet as soon as possible to try to prevent further symptoms. If your symptoms are very severe or do not improve, you should discuss this with your doctor.

breakfasts

homemade muesli

Preparation time **5 minutes**
Cooking time **30 minutes**,
  plus cooling
Serves **4**

1¼ cups **shredded dried
  coconut**
2½ cups **buckwheat flakes**
2½ cups **millet flakes**
1 cup **slivered almonds**
⅔ cup **blanched hazelnuts**
¾ cup **sunflower seeds**
4 oz **dried mango**, sliced
⅔ cup **golden raisins**

Spread the coconut out in a thin layer on a baking sheet. Toast in a preheated oven, 300°F for about 20 minutes, stirring every 5 minutes to make sure it browns evenly. Toast the slivered almonds, hazelnuts, and sunflower seeds in the same way.

Mix together all the ingredients in a large bowl until well combined. Store in an airtight container for up to 1–2 weeks.

For Bircher muesli, mix together the millet flakes, dried mango, and golden raisins, with 1 cored and grated red apple in a large bowl. Pour over 1¼ cups apple juice, cover, and chill overnight. Stir in 1½ cups toasted and roughly chopped mixed nuts, ½ cup plain yogurt and a good drizzle of honey before serving.

granola with berry compote

Preparation time **10 minutes**,
plus cooling
Cooking time **35 minutes**
Serves **4**

2 cups **buckwheat flakes**
3 tablespoons **sunflower seeds**, toasted
4 tablespoons **pumpkin seeds**, toasted
3 tablespoons **sesame seeds**, toasted
2 tablespoons **flax seeds**
²/₃ cup **mixed nuts**, roughly chopped
3 tablespoons **honey**
2 tablespoons **sunflower oil**
¹/₃ cup **ready-to-eat dried apricots**, sliced
handful of **dried blueberries**
handful of **dried cranberries**
4 oz **fresh blueberries**
4 oz **fresh strawberries**, hulled
1 tablespoon **caster sugar**
4 fl oz **yogurt**

Mix together the buckwheat flakes, all the seeds, and the nuts in a large bowl. Gently heat the honey and oil in a small saucepan, then pour into the bowl and stir to coat the mixture.

Spread the granola on a baking sheet and cook in a preheated oven, 300°F, for about 30 minutes.

Remove from the oven and break up any large lumps. Place in a large bowl and stir in all the dried fruits. Allow to cool, then store in an airtight container for up to 1–2 weeks.

Put the blueberries and strawberries in a saucepan with the sugar and a little water and gently simmer for about 5 minutes until softened. Leave to cool. To serve, divide the compote between serving bowls, top with the yogurt and sprinkle with the granola.

For orange & apricot compote, to serve as an accompaniment, put 1 cup ready-to-eat dried apricots, the juice and grated zest of 2 oranges, 1 cinnamon stick, ²/₃ cup black tea, and 2 tablespoons honey into a saucepan, bring to a gentle simmer for 10 minutes, then cool. Remove the cinnamon stick, place in a food processor or blender and blitz until smooth.

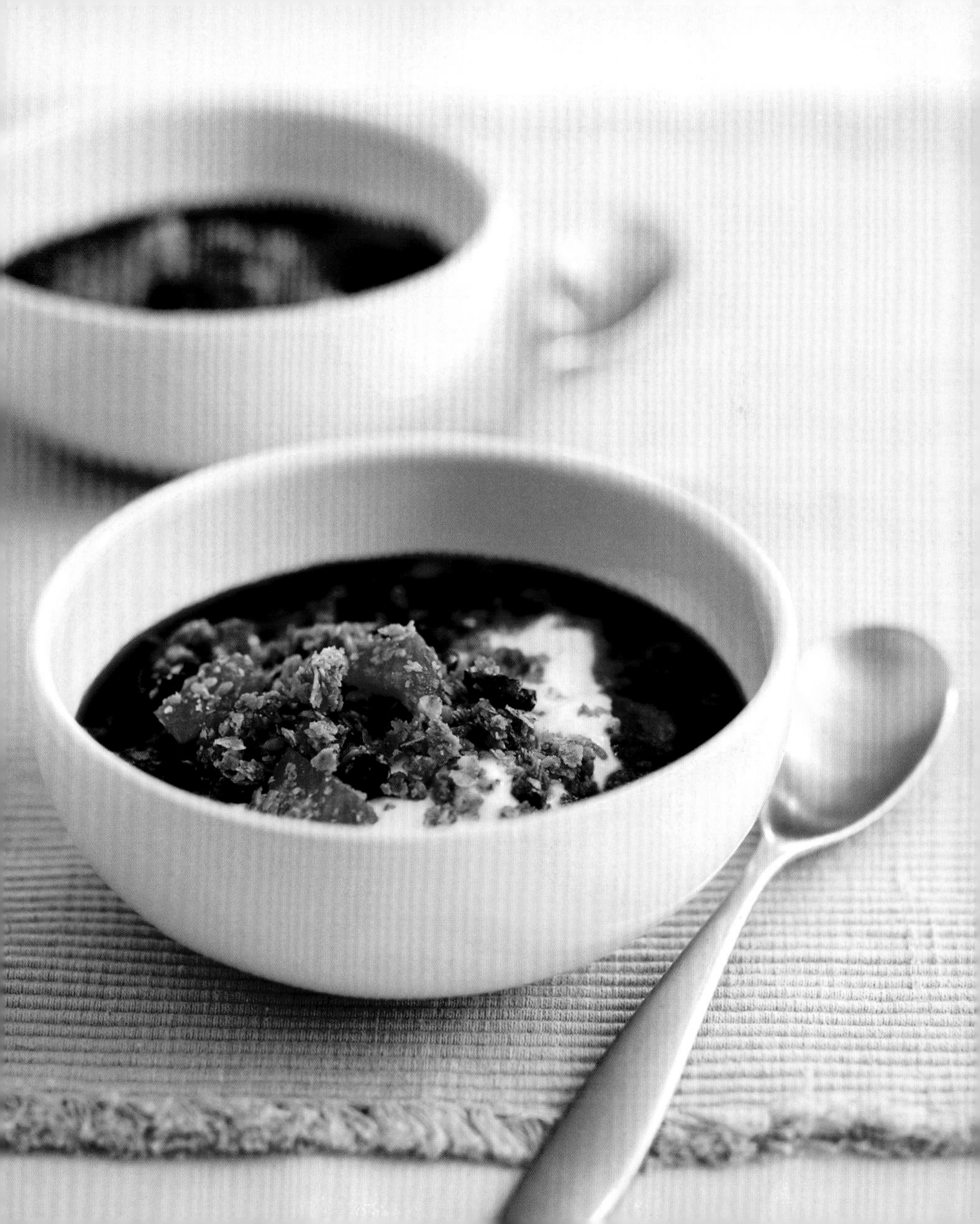

breakfast cereal bars

Preparation time **10 minutes**
Cooking time **35 minutes**
Makes **16**

½ cup **butter**, softened, plus
  extra for greasing
2 tablespoons **soft light
  brown sugar**
2 tablespoons **corn syrup**
1¼ cups **millet flakes**
⅓ cup **quinoa**
1 cup **dried cherries** or
  cranberries
½ cup **golden raisins**
3 tablespoons **sunflower
  seeds**
3 tablespoons **sesame seeds**
3 tablespoons **flax seeds**
½ cup **unsweetened
  shredded coconut**
2 **eggs**, lightly beaten

Grease an 11 x 8 inch shallow baking pan.

Beat together the butter, sugar, and syrup in a large bowl until creamy. Add all the remaining ingredients and beat well until combined.

Spoon the mixture into the prepared pan, level the surface with the back of a dessertspoon and place in a preheated oven, 350°F, for 35 minutes until deep golden. Remove from the oven and leave to cool in the pan.

Turn out onto a wooden board and carefully cut into 16 fingers using a serrated knife. Store in an airtight container for up to 5 days.

For yogurty crunch, slice 2 bananas and divide half the slices between 4 tall glasses. Mix together 1¼ cups plain yogurt and 4 tablespoons honey in a bowl and spoon half the mixture over the slices. Crumble 4 Breakfast Cereal Bars (see above) and sprinkle half over the yogurt mixture. Repeat the layering, chill, and serve.

french toasts

Preparation time **5 minutes**
Cooking time **5 minutes**
Serves **4**

2 **eggs**, beaten
1 teaspoon **vanilla extract**
½ cup **milk**
1 tablespoon **superfine sugar**, plus extra for sprinkling
½ teaspoon **ground cinnamon**
4 thick slices of **gluten-free bread**
2 tablespoons **butter**

Whisk together the eggs, vanilla extract, milk, sugar, and cinnamon in a shallow dish. Place the slices of bread in the mixture, turning to coat both sides so that they absorb the liquid.

Heat the butter in a nonstick skillet. Use a spatula to remove the soaked bread from the dish and fry the slices for 2 minutes on each side until golden. Cut the toasts in half diagonally into triangles, sprinkle with a little superfine sugar and serve.

For applesauce & raspberries, to serve as an accompaniment, heat 2 tablespoons butter in a skillet, add 6 cored and sliced dessert apples, and fry for 2–3 minutes. Sprinkle over 1 tablespoon light brown sugar, ½ teaspoon ground cinnamon and 4 oz raspberries and cook gently for 1–2 minutes. Serve over the toasts sprinkled with extra superfine sugar.

mini tomato & feta omelets

Preparation time **10 minutes**
Cooking time **10 minutes**
Makes **12**

melted **butter**, for greasing
4 **eggs**, beaten
2 tablespoons **chopped chives**
3 **sundried tomatoes**, finely sliced
3 oz **feta cheese**, crumbled
salt and **black pepper**

Brush a 12-cup mini muffin pan lightly with melted butter to grease.

Mix together all the remaining ingredients in a large bowl until just combined.

Pour the mixture into the greased holes and place in a preheated oven, 425°F, for about 10 minutes until golden and puffed up. Remove from the oven and serve warm.

For pea, bacon, & Parmesan omelets, broil 4 bacon slices until crisp, then chop. Whisk together the eggs, 2 tablespoons grated Parmesan cheese, 1 tablespoon chopped parsley, and 1 tablespoon gluten-free whole grain mustard in a large bowl. Stir in the bacon and 2 tablespoons peas, thawed if frozen. Pour into the prepared muffin pan and cook as above.

kedgeree

Preparation time **10 minutes**
Cooking time **20 minutes**
Serves **4**

1 cup **basmati rice**
1 lb **skinless smoked
   haddock fillets**
2 **bay leaves**
¼ cup **butter**
1 **onion**, chopped
1 **garlic clove**, crushed
2 tablespoons **curry powder**
4 **scallions**, finely sliced
handful of **cilantro**, chopped
2 **hard-cooked eggs**, roughly
   chopped
salt and black pepper

Cook the basmati rice in a saucepan of salted boiling water according to the package instructions. Drain well.

Place the haddock in a skillet with the bay leaves, just cover with water, then simmer for 5–6 minutes until it is just cooked. Drain and flake.

Meanwhile, heat the butter in a pan, add the onion and garlic and fry for 4–5 minutes until softened. Add the curry powder and continue to fry for 1 minute.

Stir in the rice, haddock, scallions, cilantro, and eggs. Season well with black pepper and heat through until piping hot. Serve immediately.

For shrimp & pea kedgeree, omit the haddock and fry the onion and garlic with ½ seeded and sliced red chili as above. Add the curry powder and fry for a minute more. Stir in 3 cups cooked basmati rice, 10 oz cooked peeled prawns, 1 cup peas, thawed if frozen, 2 tablespoons chopped mint, and the grated zest and juice of ½ lemon. Heat through until piping hot and season well.

hash breakfast

Preparation time **10 minutes**
Cooking time **10 minutes**
Serves **4**

2 tablespoons **olive oil**
1 **onion**, chopped
1 lb cooked **potatoes**, cubed
11½ oz can **corned beef**,
   roughly chopped
dash of **Worcestershire sauce**
4 **eggs**
black pepper

To garnish
chopped **parsley**, to garnish
pinch **smoked paprika**, to
   garnish

Heat half the oil in a large skillet, add the onion and potatoes, and fry for 5–6 minutes or until the potatoes are golden and the onions are softened.

Stir in the corned beef and season well with pepper and Worcestershire sauce. Continue to fry for 2–3 minutes.

Meanwhile, heat the remaining oil in a skillet pan and fry the eggs.

Spoon the hash onto 4 serving plates, top each with a fried egg and serve sprinkled with the chopped parsley and a little smoked paprika.

For breakfast in a pan, heat all the olive oil in a large skillet, add 1 lb chopped gluten-free sausages, and fry for 3–4 minutes until browned and almost cooked through. Add the potatoes and continue to cook for 2–3 minutes until beginning to brown. Stir in a handful of halved cherry tomatoes and 4 sliced scallions, spread out evenly in the pan, then crack in the eggs and cook for 1–2 minutes. Cut into 4 and serve.

potato pancakes

Preparation time **10 minutes**
Cooking time **20–25 minutes**
Serves **4**

1 lb 2 oz large **potatoes**,
  peeled and cut into
  small chunks
1½ teaspoons **gluten-free**
  baking powder
2 medium **eggs**
5 tablespoons **whole milk**
vegetable oil, for frying
salt and **black pepper**

Cook the potatoes in a saucepan of salted boiling water for 15 minutes or until tender. Drain well, return to the pan, and mash until smooth. Allow to cool slightly.

Beat in the baking powder, then the eggs, milk, and a little salt and pepper, and continue to beat until everything is evenly combined.

Heat a little oil in a heavy skillet. Drop heaped dessertspoonfuls of the mixture into the pan, spacing them slightly apart, and fry for 3–4 minutes, turning once, until golden. Transfer to a serving plate and keep warm while frying the remainder of the potato mixture.

Serve warm, instead of toast, with your favourite cooked breakfast.

For salmon & potato pancakes, add 100 g 4 oz chopped smoked salmon, 2 tablespoons snipped chives, and 3 sliced scallions to the potato mixture and cook as above.

yogurt & berry smoothie

Preparation time **5 minutes**
Serves **4**

1¼ cups **plain yogurt**
3 cups fresh or frozen **mixed
    summer berries**, thawed if
    frozen, plus extra to decorate
4 tablespoons **millet flakes**
3 tablespoons **honey**
1¼ cups **cranberry juice**

Place all the ingredients in a food processor or a blender and blitz until smooth.

Pour into 4 glasses, decorate wth a few extra whole berries and serve immediately.

For frozen raspberry yogurt slice, blitz 3 cups raspberries, 1¾ cups confectioners' sugar, the juice of 1 lemon, and 2½ cups whole milk yogurt in a food processor or blender. Pour the mixture into a 2 lb loaf pan that has been lined with plastic wrap, then freeze until solid. Serve sliced with mixed berries.

tropical fruit smoothie

Preparation time **10 minutes**
Serves **4**

1 **mango**, peeled, pitted,
  and chopped
2 **kiwifruits**, peeled and
  chopped
1 **banana**, cut into chunks
14 oz can **pineapple chunks**
  in natural juice
1¾ cups **orange** or **apple**
  juice
handful of **ice cubes**

Place all the ingredients in a food processor or blender and blitz until smooth.

Pour into 4 glasses and serve immediately.

For tropical cocktail, blitz all the above ingredients in a food processor or blender with 1¾ cups coconut milk and 6 tablespoons white rum. Serve in 4 glasses over ice.

lunches &
light bites

tomato & chorizo soup

Preparation time **10 minutes**
Cooking time **25 minutes**
Serves **4**

1 lb **red bell peppers**, halved
  and seeded
2 tablespoons **olive oil**
1 large **onion**, chopped
2 **garlic cloves**, crushed
5 oz **chorizo sausage**, sliced
1 teaspoon **ground cumin**
1 teaspoon **smoked paprika**
1 lb **tomatoes**, halved and
  deseeded
2½ cups **gluten-free chicken**
  or **vegetable stock**
handful of **parsley**, chopped
salt and **black pepper**

Put the red peppers on a baking sheet. Drizzle over half the olive oil and roast in a preheated oven, 400°F, for 10–15 minutes, turning after 5 minutes.

Heat the remaining olive oil in a large saucepan while the peppers are roasting, and add the onion, garlic, and chorizo and fry for 3–4 minutes until the onion is softened and the chorizo is beginning to brown. Stir in the spices and fry for 1 minute.

Add the tomatoes and the stock to the saucepan and season well. Bring to a boil and simmer for 5 minutes.

Remove the peppers from the oven, skin and roughly chop the flesh. Add to the soup and simmer for a further 15 minutes.

Remove from the heat and allow to cool for 5 minutes. Roughly blend in a food processor or blender, if desired, then stir in the parsley and serve.

For tomato soup with creamy basil, omit the red peppers and fry the onion and garlic as above, replacing the chorizo and spices with 1 chopped carrot and 1 chopped celery stalk. Add the tomatoes and vegetable stock, bring to a boil and simmer for 25 minutes. Purée in a food processor or blender until smooth. Return to the pan and stir in 2 tablespoons mascarpone cheese and 1 tablespoon pesto. Season and serve.

thai vegetable, tofu, & rice soup

Preparation time **15 minutes**
Cooking time **20 minutes**
Serves **4**

5 cups **gluten-free vegetable stock**
2 **lemon grass stalks**, halved and bruised
2 **garlic cloves**, finely sliced
handful of **cilantro**, stalks finely chopped and leaves torn
2 **Kaffir lime leaves**
2 **red chilies**, seeded and halved
2 inch **fresh ginger**, peeled and halved
¾ cup sliced **green beans**, topped and tailed, then sliced
7½ oz can **water chestnuts**, drained and sliced
7 oz **firm tofu**, cubed
²/₃ cup **coconut cream**
4 **scallions**, sliced
1 cup **basmati rice**

Pour the stock into a large saucepan, stir in the lemon grass, garlic, cilantro stalks, lime leaves, chilies, and ginger and simmer for 10 minutes. Remove the pieces of ginger and lemon grass.

Add the beans, water chestnuts, tofu, and coconut cream and simmer until the beans are just tender. Meanwhile cook the basmati rice in a saucepan of boiling water according to the package instructions.

Drain the rice, then add half the rice and the scallions to the soup and heat through until piping hot.

Sprinkle the remaining cilantro leaves over the soup, ladle into bowls and garnish with the remaining chili, finely sliced. Serve with an extra dish of the remaining rice for each person.

For Thai chicken noodle soup, make the soup as above, replacing the tofu with 10 oz cooked and shredded chicken and 1 seeded and finely sliced red bell pepper. Omit the rice and replace with 7 oz cooked rice noodles.

sweet potato, squash, & coconut soup

Preparation time **10 minutes**
Cooking time **40–45 minutes**
Serves **4**

2 large **sweet potatoes**,
  peeled and cut into chunks
1 large **butternut squash**,
  peeled, seeded, and cut
  into chunks
1 **onion**, cut into wedges
2 **garlic cloves**, peeled
1 teaspoon **cumin seeds**
2 tablespoons **olive oil**
½ teaspoon **dried red pepper
  flakes**, plus extra to garnish
  (optional)
3 ⅔ cups **gluten-free
  vegetable stock**
¾ cup **coconut cream**
1 teaspoon **garam masala**
salt and **black pepper**

Put the sweet potatoes, squash, onion, and garlic on a baking sheet. Sprinkle over the cumin seeds and drizzle with the oil. Place in a preheated oven, 400°F, and roast for 25–30 minutes until tender and golden.

Tip the roasted vegetables into a large saucepan with the pepper flakes and stock, bring to a boil, and simmer for 10 minutes.

Stir in the remaining ingredients, heat through until piping hot and then purée in a food processor or blender until smooth. Serve, garnished with a pinch of chili flakes if liked, and with toasted gluten-free bread.

For squash & lentil soup, roast the squash, onion, and garlic as above, omitting the sweet potatoes, for 20 minutes until nearly cooked. Transfer to a large saucepan and add 3½ oz split red lentils (rinsed and drained), and 5 cups gluten-free vegetable stock. Bring to a boil and simmer for about 25 minutes until the lentils and squash are soft. Purée in a food processor or blender until smooth and season well with salt and pepper. Serve with warm crusty gluten-free bread.

mexican bean soup

Preparation time **10 minutes**
Cooking time **30 minutes**
Serves **4**

1 tablespoon **olive oil**
1 **onion**, chopped
1 **garlic clove**, crushed
1 **red chili**, seeded and
  chopped
bunch of **cilantro**, stalks and
  leaves chopped separately
1 **green bell pepper**, cored,
  seeded and chopped
1 teaspoon **ground cumin**
1 teaspoon **smoked paprika**
2 x 13 oz cans **black-eyed
  peas**, drained and rinsed
13 oz can **chopped tomatoes**
2 tablespoons **sundried
  tomato paste**
2½ cups **gluten-free
  vegetable stock**
salt and **black pepper**

Heat the oil in a large saucepan, add the onion, garlic, and chili and fry for 2 minutes. Add the cilantro stalks and green pepper and continue to fry for 2–3 minutes, then stir in the cumin and paprika.

Stir in the beans, tomatoes, tomato paste, and stock, bring to a boil and simmer for 20 minutes.

Purée half the soup in a food processor or blender, then return to the pan with the cilantro leaves (reserving 4 for garnish), season well with salt and pepper, and heat through until piping hot. Serve garnished with the reserved cilantro leaves.

For guacamole, to serve as an accompaniment, roughly mash 1 stoned and peeled large ripe avocado with the juice of 1 lime in a bowl. Stir in ½ cup chopped tomatoes, 4 sliced scallions, a handful of chopped cilantro, 1 small seeded and chopped red chili and a good seasoning of salt. Add a spoonful of the guacamole to the soup before serving.

fish chowder

Preparation time **10 minutes**
Cooking time **30 minutes**
Serves **4**

1 tablespoon **butter**
1 tablespoon **vegetable oil**
1 **onion**, finely chopped
4 oz **bacon**, chopped
2 tablespoons **cornstarch**
2½ cups **gluten-free fish stock**
2½ cups **milk**
1 lb **floury potatoes**, peeled and cubed
1 lb mixed **skinless firm white fish fillets**, cubed
10 oz **skinless smoked haddock fillets**, cubed
8 oz **raw shrimp**, peeled and deveined
⅔ cup **light cream**
salt and **black pepper**
chopped **parsley**, to garnish

Heat the butter and oil in a large saucepan, add the onion, and fry for 3 minutes until softened. Add the bacon and fry for 3–4 minutes more until beginning to brown.

Add in the cornstarch and cook, stirring, for 1 minute then gradually add the stock and milk and cook, stirring all the time, until thickened and smooth. Mix in the potatoes and simmer for 10 minutes, then add the fish and cook gently for 5–6 minutes more until just cooked through.

Mix in the shrimp and cream and cook gently until the shrimp are cooked through and piping hot. Season well, ladle into bowls, and serve sprinkled with chopped parsley.

For spiced corn chowder, fry the onion as above, adding 1 seeded and chopped red chili. Omit the bacon. Stir in the cornstarch, and then gradually stir in 2½ cups gluten-free vegetable stock and the milk as above. Mix in 1¼ lb peeled and chopped potatoes and 2 x 7 oz cans drained corn kernels and simmer until the potato is tender. Season well, ladle into bowls, and sprinkle with a handful of chopped parsley or cilantro.

chicken & ham soup

Preparation time **20 minutes**
Cooking time **1 hour 20
minutes**
Serves **8**

12 oz piece of **lean
uncooked ham**
3 tablespoons **olive oil**
4 large **skinless chicken
thighs**
3 **onions**, chopped
2 **celery sticks**, sliced
2 **bay leaves**
2½ cups **gluten-free
chicken stock**
12 oz **potatoes**, peeled and
cut into small dice
1 cup **frozen sweetcorn**

Dumplings
¾ cup **fine cornmeal**
1 cup **gluten-free flour**
2 teaspoons **gluten-free
baking powder**
1 tablespoon chopped **thyme**
3 tablespoons chilled **butter**
salt and **black pepper**

Chop the ham into ½ inch chunks. Heat the oil in a large heavy saucepan, add the chicken, onions, and celery and fry gently for 10 minutes, stirring until golden.

Add the ham, bay leaves, stock, and 2½ cups water and bring to a boil. Reduce the heat, cover, and simmer gently for 40 minutes until the chicken and ham are tender.

Lift out the chicken with a slotted spoon and, when cool enough to handle, shred the flesh from the bones. Return the flesh to the pan with the potatoes and corn. Simmer, covered, for 20 minutes, until the potatoes are tender.

Make the dumplings. Mix together the cornmeal, flour, baking powder, thyme, and salt and pepper in a bowl until evenly combined. Grate the butter into the mixture and add 1 cup water. Mix to a thick paste, adding a little more water if necessary.

Use 2 dessertspoons to roughly pat the paste into 8 rounds and spoon into the soup. Cover and simmer gently for about 10 minutes until the dumplings are light and puffy.

For pea & ham soup, place 1 cup rinsed and drained yellow split peas, 4 cups water, 3 oz chopped smoked ham, 1 large chopped carrot, 1 chopped onion, and 2 bay leaves into a large saucepan, bring to a boil, removing any scum that comes to the surface, cover and simmer for 40 minutes until the split peas are tender. Purée in a food processor or blender, season well and serve sprinkled with chopped parsley.

chilled gazpacho

Preparation time **20 minutes**, plus chilling
Serves **6**

1¾ lb **tomatoes**, skinned and roughly chopped
½ **cucumber**, roughly chopped
2 **red bell peppers**, cored, deseeded, and roughly chopped
1 **celery stick**, chopped
2 **garlic cloves**, chopped
½ red chili, seeded and sliced
small handful of **cilantro**
2 tablespoons **white wine vinegar**
2 tablespoons **sundried tomato paste**
4 tablespoons **olive oil**
salt
ice cubes, to serve

Mix together the vegetables, garlic, chili, and cilantro in a large bowl. Add the vinegar, tomato paste, oil, and a little salt.

Blitz in batches in a food processor or blender until smooth, scraping the mixture down from the side of the bowl if necessary.

Collect the blended mixtures together in a clean bowl and check the seasoning, adding a little more salt if needed. Cover and chill for up to 24 hours.

When ready to serve, ladle the gazpacho into large bowls, and sprinkle with ice cubes. Serve with crackers or slices of chorizo sausage.

For gazpacho topping, to serve as an accompaniment, heat 2 tablespoons olive oil in a skillet, add 3 cups gluten-free bread cubes, and fry until golden. Place the croutons in a bowl and stir in 2 sliced scallions, 1 cored, deseeded, and finely sliced green bell pepper, 2 roughly chopped hard-cooked eggs, and a handful of chopped cilantro. Sprinkle over the gazpacho before serving.

chickpea & feta salad

Preparation time **10 minutes**
Cooking time **10–15 minutes**
Serves **4**

4 tablespoons **olive oil**
1 lb **red bell peppers**, halved, cored and deseeded
2 x 13 oz cans **chickpeas**, drained, and rinsed
5 oz **feta cheese**, crumbled
1 **red chili**, seeded and finely sliced
2 cups **arugula leaves** or **baby leaf spinach**
8 **cherry tomatoes**, quartered
handful of **mint**, chopped
handful of **cilantro**, chopped
drizzle of **red wine vinegar**
black pepper

Put the red peppers on a baking sheet and drizzle over half the olive oil. Place in a preheated oven, 400°F, for 10–15 minutes, turning after 5 minutes.

Remove from the oven, peel off the skins and slice the flesh. Place in a large serving bowl. Add the chickpeas, feta, chili, arugula leaves or spinach, tomatoes, and herbs to the serving bowl and mix together with a large spoon.

Drizzle the remaining olive oil over the salad, add the red wine vinegar, season with pepper and gently mix.

Serve the salad with grilled meats or fish, or with warmed gluten-free pitta bread.

For lentil & tomato salad with crispy bacon, cook 1¼ cups Puy lentils in a saucepan of boiling water according to the package instructions then drain well. Whisk together 2 tablespoons olive oil, 2 teaspoons gluten-free Dijon mustard, 2 teaspoons honey, 1 tablespoon balsamic vinegar, and a handful of chopped fresh herbs in a bowl. Stir in the warm lentils with 2 large handfuls of baby leaf spinach, 1 cup sundried tomatoes in oil, and 4 oz crumbled soft goats' cheese. Broil 6 bacon slices until brown and crisp, cool a little, then roughly chop and sprinkle over the salad.

potato & avocado salad

Preparation time **10 minutes**
Cooking time **12–15 minutes**
Serves **4**

1 ¼ lb small **new potatoes**
1 ripe **avocado**
1 container **mustard and
  cress**
grated zest of ½ **lemon**
2 cups **arugula leaves**
salt and **black pepper**

Dressing
1 tablespoon **gluten-free
  whole grain mustard**
juice of ½ **lemon**
2 tablespoons **mayonnaise**

Cook the potatoes in a saucepan of salted boiling
water for 12–15 minutes or until just tender.

Drain well and place in a large salad bowl.

Halve the avocado and remove the stone. Cut the flesh
into pieces. Whisk together the dressing ingredients in
a small bowl, then add to the warm potatoes. Mix in
the avocado pieces, cress, lemon zest, and arugula.
Season well.

Divide the salad between 4 plates and serve.

For potato & sundried tomato salad, cook the
potatoes as above, drain well, and place in a large salad
bowl. While they are still warm, stir in 6 sliced, drained
sundried tomatoes in oil, 12 sliced pitted olives,
2 tablespoons pesto and 3 tablespoons light sour
cream. Season with plenty of black pepper.

roasted veggie & quinoa salad

Preparation time **5 minutes**
Cooking time **20–25 minutes**
Serves **4**

3 **zucchini**, cut into chunks
2 **red bell peppers**, cored,
   seeded, and cut into chunks
2 **red onions**, cut into wedges
1 large **eggplant**, cut into
   chunks
3 **garlic cloves**, peeled
3 tablespoons **olive oil**
¾ cup **quinoa**
2 tablespoons **green pesto** or
   sundried tomato paste
1 tablespoon **balsamic
   vinegar**
2 cups **arugula leaves**

Put all the vegetables and garlic on a large baking sheet and drizzle over the olive oil. Place in a preheated oven, 425°F, for 20–25 minutes until tender and beginning to char.

Meanwhile, cook the quinoa in a saucepan of boiling water according to the package instructions, then drain well.

Whisk together the pesto or tomato paste and balsamic vinegar in a small bowl. Place the roasted vegetables, arugula, and quinoa in a large serving bowl and stir in the dressing. Serve warm.

For quinoa with salmon & watercress, cook the quinoa as above. Meanwhile, place 2 large pieces of skinless salmon fillet, about 10 oz total weight, in a nonstick skillet and cook for 3 minutes on each side until crisp and just cooked through, then flake. Whisk together ¾ cup light sour cream, the grated zest and juice of 1 orange, and 1 tablespoon gluten-free whole grain mustard in a small bowl. Stir the dressing into the quinoa with the flaked salmon and a bunch of chopped watercress.

italian bread salad

Preparation time **10 minutes,**
plus standing
Cooking time **10 minutes**
Serves **4**

2 **red bell peppers,**
deseeded, and sliced
3 tablespoons **olive oil**
1 lb 5 oz **tomatoes**, skinned
and chopped
1 **red onion**, finely sliced
handful of **green olives**
1 tablespoon **capers**, rinsed
1 **red chili**, seeded and
finely chopped
handful of **basil leaves**
2 tablespoons **red wine**
vinegar
4 tablespoons **olive oil**
7 oz **gluten-free bread**, cubed
and toasted
salt and **black pepper**

Put the red peppers on a baking sheet, drizzle over half
the olive oil and place in a preheated oven, 400°F, for
10 minutes, turning after 5 minutes. Leave to cool then
remove the skin.

Mix together all the remaining ingredients apart from
the toasted bread cubes in a large bowl, and set aside
for at least 20 minutes to allow the flavors to develop.

Add the red peppers to the bowl when cooled. Just
before serving, add the toasted bread cubes, stir, then
serve with grilled meats.

For Mediterranean vegetable & chicken pasta,
roast the red peppers as above. Meanwhile, cook
12 oz gluten-free pasta shapes in a saucepan of salted
boiling water according to the package instructions.
Mix together with the remaining ingredients, reserving
1 tablespoon of the oil. While the peppers and pasta
are cooking, mix together 1 crushed garlic clove,
1 tablespoon olive oil, 1 tablespoon thyme leaves, and
1 teaspoon balsamic vinegar and pour over 4 sliced
boneless, skinless chicken breasts in a dish. Cover and
leave to marinate for 10 minutes. Drain the pasta well,
put in a large bowl and mix with the roasted red peppers
and all the other ingredients as above but only using
3 tablespoons of the olive oil. Heat a griddle pan until
hot and cook the chicken for 2–3 minutes on each
side until cooked through, then serve on top of the
vegetable pasta.

walnut, pear, & green leaf salad

Preparation time **10 minutes**
Cooking time **2–3 minutes**
Serves **4**

vegetable oil, for greasing
¾ cup grated **Parmesan cheese**
2 large ripe **pears**
½ cup **walnut pieces**, lightly toasted
1 ½ cup **mixed leaf salad**

Dressing
6 tablespoons **walnut oil**
2 tablespoons **lemon juice**
1 tablespoon **gluten-free whole grain mustard**
2 teaspoons **superfine sugar**
several sprigs of **tarragon**, roughly chopped
salt and **black pepper**

Oil a foil-lined baking sheet and sprinkle the Parmesan over it, spreading it into a thin layer about 10 inches square. Cook under a hot broiler for 2–3 minutes until the cheese has melted and is pale golden. Leave until cool enough to handle, then peel the foil away, letting the cheese break into pieces to form 'croûtes.'

Whisk together the dressing ingredients in a large bowl. Halve and core the pears then cut into thin slices.

Add the pears, walnuts, and salad leaves to the bowl with the dressing and toss together. Pile onto 4 serving plates and sprinkle with the Parmesan croutes.

For blue cheese & pear salad, whisk together 1 tablespoon sweet chili sauce, 1 tablespoon olive oil, and 1 tablespoon red wine vinegar in a small bowl. Mix together 2½ cups arugula leaves, 2 sliced heads of Belgian endive, 1 pear, cored and sliced, 1 cup walnut pieces, and 4 oz crumbled blue cheese in a large serving bowl, drizzle over the dressing, and serve.

goat cheese & onion tarts

Preparation time **15 minutes,**
plus chilling
Cooking time **12–15 minutes**
Serves **4**

²/₃ cup **rice flour**, plus extra
for dusting
1 tablespoon **cornmeal**
¹/₃ cup **butter**, cubed
1 tablespoon grated
Parmesan cheese
1 **egg yolk**

Filling
2 tablespoons **onion
marmalade** or **chutney**
3 oz **soft goat cheese**,
crumbled
1 teaspoon **thyme leaves**

Place the rice flour, cornmeal, butter, and Parmesan in a food processor and whiz until the mixture resembles fine bread crumbs or blend by hand in a large bowl. Alternatively, mix together the rice flour and cornmeal in a bowl. Add the butter and rub in with the fingertips until the mix resembles fine bread crumbs. Stir in the Parmesan.

Add the egg yolk and enough cold water to form a soft but not sticky dough. Wrap in plastic wrap and chill for 30 minutes.

Roll the dough out on a surface lightly dusted with rice flour and use a 4 inch plain cutter to stamp out 4 rounds, rerolling the trimmings as necessary.

Put the pastry rounds on a baking sheet lightly dusted with rice flour, then spoon over the onion marmalade or chutney, dot with the goat cheese, and sprinkle with the thyme.

Place in a preheated oven, 400°F, for 12–15 minutes until golden. Serve with a spinach and arugula leaf salad, if liked.

For Mediterranean tarts, make the pastry as above and spoon 1 teaspoon sundried tomato paste over the pastry rounds. Grill, skin, seed, and slice 1 red bell pepper, then mix together with 12 black olives, 4 oz crumbled feta cheese, and 3 drained and sliced bottled artichoke hearts. Divide between the pastries, then bake as above.

crab cakes ·

Preparation time **15 minutes,
plus chilling**
Cooking time **20 minutes**
Serves **4**

10 oz **potatoes**, peeled and
 chopped
12 oz **fresh white crabmeat**
3 **scallions**, sliced
handful of **cilantro**, leaves and
 stalks finely chopped
good squeeze of **lime juice**
½ **chili**, seeded and finely
 chopped
1 **egg yolk**
3 tablespoons **cornmeal**
2 tablespoons **vegetable oil**
salt and **black pepper**

To serve
lime wedges
mixed leaf salad

Cook the potatoes in a saucepan of salted boiling
water for 15 minutes or until tender. Drain well, return
to the pan and mash. Leave to cool. Stir in all the
remaining ingredients except the cornmeal and oil.

Put the cornmeal on a plate, shape the crab mixture
into 8 cakes and coat in the cornmeal. Cover and chill
for 20 minutes.

Heat the oil in a large skillet, add the cakes and fry for
2–3 minutes on each side until golden. Serve with lime
wedges and a mixed leaf salad.

For chili dipping sauce, to serve as an accompaniment,
place ⅓ cup superfine sugar and 4 tablespoons water
in a saucepan, heat until the sugar has dissolved, then
bubble until it turns a caramel color. Stir in 2 seeded and
chopped red chilies, 1 sliced lemon grass stalk, 1 sliced
garlic clove, the grated zest and juice of 1 lime, and 1
tablespoon peeled and finely shredded fresh ginger
root. Pour into a serving dish and allow to cool.

sweet potatoes with tomato salsa

Preparation time **5 minutes**
Cooking time **45 minutes**
Serves **4**

4 large **sweet potatoes**, about
  9 oz each
2 tablespoons **olive oil**
4 oz **Emmental** or **cheddar
  cheese**, grated
salt

Salsa
4 large **tomatoes**
1 small **red onion**, finely
  chopped
2 **celery sticks**, finely chopped
handful of **cilantro**, chopped
4 tablespoons **lime juice**
4 teaspoons **superfine sugar**

Scrub the potatoes and put them in a small roasting pan. Prick with a fork, drizzle with the oil and sprinkle with a little salt. Place in a preheated oven, 400°F, for 45 minutes until tender.

Meanwhile, make the salsa. Finely chop the tomatoes and mix with the onion, celery, cilantro, lime juice, and sugar in a bowl.

Halve the potatoes and fluff up the flesh with a fork. Sprinkle with the cheese and top with the salsa. Serve with a green salad.

For baked sweet potatoes with citrus spiced butter, cook the sweet potatoes as above. Meanwhile, beat together ¼ cup softened butter, ½ teaspoon red pepper flakes, the grated zest of 1 orange, and 2 tablespoons chopped cilantro in a small bowl. Spoon onto the halved baked potatoes and serve with griddled chicken, if desired.

quick nachos

Preparation time **5 minutes**
Cooking time **1–2 minutes**
Serves **4**

7 oz **gluten-free plain corn tortilla chips**
1¼ cups **ready-made fresh tomato salsa**
1 cup grated **Monterey Jack** or **Cheddar cheese**
handful of **cilantro,** chopped
sour cream, to serve

Put the tortilla chips into a wide ovenproof dish. Spoon over the tomato salsa, then sprinkle with the grated cheese and cilantro.

Place under a medium broiler and cook for 1–2 minutes until the cheese is golden and bubbling. Serve with sour cream.

For chili beef nachos, heat 1 tablespoon olive oil in a skillet, add 1 chopped onion, 1 crushed garlic clove, and 1 seeded and sliced red chili and fry for 2–3 minutes. Add 10 oz lean ground beef and fry for 2–3 minutes until browned. Stir in the tomato salsa as above and a 13 oz can drained kidney beans and simmer for 20 minutes. Spoon the mixture over the tortilla chips in an ovenproof dish, sprinkle with the cheese, then place under the broiler as above.

spinach, tomato, & parmesan scones

Preparation time **10 minutes**
Cooking time **12–15 minutes**
Makes **8**

1 cup **rice flour**, plus extra for
dusting
½ cup **cornstarch**
1 teaspoon **gluten-free
baking powder**
1 teaspoon **baking soda**
⅓ cup **butter**, cubed
½ cup **frozen leaf spinach**,
thawed, squeezed of any
liquid, and chopped
4 **sundried tomatoes in oil**,
drained and finely chopped
½ cup grated **Parmesan
cheese**,
good grating of **nutmeg**
1 large **egg**, beaten
3 tablespoons **buttermilk**, plus
extra for brushing

Place the rice flour, cornstarch, baking powder, baking
soda, and butter in a food processor and whiz until the
mixture resembles fine bread crumbs. Alternatively, mix
together the dry ingredients in a large bowl. Add the
butter and rub in with the fingertips until the mixture
resembles fine bread crumbs. Mix in the spinach,
sundried tomatoes, Parmesan, and nutmeg.

Whisk together the egg and buttermilk, with a fork in a
separate bowl, stir into the flour mixture and combine to
form a soft dough.

Turn the dough out on a surface lightly dusted with rice
flour, press out to a thickness of 1 inch, and use a 2 inch
cutter to stamp out 8 scones, rerolling the trimmings
as necessary.

Put on a baking sheet lightly dusted with rice flour,
brush with a little buttermilk, and place in a preheated
oven, 425°F, for 12–15 minutes until risen and golden.
Serve warm, spread with butter or to accompany
the soup.

For olive, feta, & herb scones, make the dough as
above, omitting the spinach, sundried tomatoes, and
nutmeg and replacing with 18 sliced pitted olives, 4 oz
crumbled feta cheese, and 1 tablespoon chopped fresh
herbs. Continue as above.

zucchini, beet, & feta fritters

Preparation time **10 minutes**
Cooking time **6–12 minutes**
Serves **4**

1 large **zucchini**, grated
grated zest of 1 **lemon**
2 **scallions**, sliced
2 tablespoons chopped
  parsley
2 tablespoons chopped **mint**
4 oz **feta cheese**, crumbled
2 tablespoons **rice flour**
1 **egg yolk**
2 cooked **beets**, peeled
  and grated
2 tablespoons **olive oil**
salt and **black pepper**
basil leaves, to garnish
mixed leaf salad, to serve

Mix together the zucchini, lemon zest, scallions, herbs, feta, rice flour, and egg yolk in a large bowl and season well. Gently stir in the beets until the mixture is just speckled with red.

Heat a little of the oil in a skillet, add tablespoons of the mixture to the pan, and fry the fritters for 1–2 minutes on each side until golden. Transfer to a serving plate and keep warm while frying the remainder of the mixture, adding the remaining oil to the pan, as necessary.

Garnish the fritters with basil leaves and a mixed leaf salad.

For a cucumber & yogurt dip, to serve as an accompaniment, mix together ¾ cup whole milk yogurt, 1 crushed garlic clove, 1 teaspoon toasted cumin seeds, ¼ grated cucumber, squeezed of excess liquid, and a pinch of paprika in a serving dish. Season well with salt and pepper.

sushi triangles

Preparation time **20 minutes**
Serves **4**

3 cups cooked **sushi rice**
sushi rice seasoning, to taste
4 sheets of **nori seaweed**
4 oz **smoked salmon**
2 oz **cucumber**, very thinly
  sliced

To serve
gluten-free soy sauce
wasabi

Season the rice to taste with the sushi rice seasoning.

Place 2 of the seaweed sheets on a board. Spread a quarter of the rice over each and cover with the smoked salmon, then the cucumber. Spoon over the remaining rice, then top with the other seaweed sheets. Press the sushi down well so that the layers stick together.

Cut into 4 triangles and serve with soy and wasabi.

For shrimp & roasted pepper sushi, season the rice as above, then layer onto the seaweed sheets with 4 oz cooked peeled shrimp, 1 sliced roasted red bell pepper, and 1 stoned, peeled, and sliced ripe avocado. Top with the remaining seaweed sheets and continue as above.

gruyère & olive pancakes

Preparation time **10 minutes**
Cooking time **6–12 minutes**
Serves **4**

1 cup **ricotta cheese**
²/₃ cup **milk**
3 **eggs**, separated
²/₃ cup **rice flour**
1 teaspoon **gluten-free baking powder**
1 tablespoon chopped **chives**
12 **pitted olives**, quartered
2 oz **Gruyère cheese**, grated
2 tablespoons grated **Parmesan cheese**
½ oz **butter**

To serve (optional)
grilled bacon rashers
cherry tomatoes, halved

Beat together the ricotta, milk, and egg yolks in a large bowl. Sift together the flour and baking powder in a separate bowl, then fold into the ricotta mixture.

Whisk the egg whites in a clean bowl until they form stiff peaks, then fold into the ricotta mixture with the chives, olives, Gruyère, and Parmesan.

Heat a little of the butter in a nonstick skillet, add spoonfuls of the mixture, and fry for 1–2 minutes on each side. Transfer to a serving plate and keep warm while frying the remainder of the mixture, adding the remaining butter to the pan, as necessary.

Serve warm with crispy bacon and halved cherry tomatoes, if desired.

For pear & cinnamon pancakes, make the pancake mixture as above, omitting the chives, olives, and cheeses. Peel, core, and roughly chop 2 ripe pears and stir into the mixture with 2 tablespoons superfine sugar and 1 teaspoon ground cinnamon. Cook as above. Serve with a drizzle of honey and a spoonful of light sour cream.

lima bean & chorizo stew

Preparation time **10 minutes**
Cooking time **20 minutes**
Serves **4**

1 tablespoon **olive oil**
1 large **onion**, chopped
2 **garlic cloves**, crushed
7 oz **chorizo sausage**, sliced
1 **green bell pepper**, cored,
    seeded, and chopped
1 **red bell pepper**, cored,
    seeded, and chopped
1 glass **red wine**
2 x 13 oz cans **lima beans**,
    drained and rinsed
13 oz can **cherry tomatoes**
1 tablespoon **tomato paste**
salt and **black pepper**
chopped **parsley**, to garnish
crusty gluten-free bread,
    to serve

Heat the oil in a flameproof casserole, add the onion and garlic and fry for 1–2 minutes. Stir in the chorizo and fry until beginning to brown. Add the peppers and fry for 3 minutes.

Pour in the wine and allow to bubble, then stir in the lima beans, tomatoes, and tomato paste and season well with salt and pepper. Cover and simmer for 15 minutes. Ladle into shallow bowls, sprinkle with the parsley to garnish, and serve with crusty gluten-free bread.

For garlic shrimp with lima beans, cook the onion and garlic as above, then stir in 10 oz raw peeled and deveined shrimp instead of the chorizo and fry until they just turn pink. Add the lima beans, 3 tablespoons light sour cream, and 2 handfuls of arugula leaves and season well. Heat through and serve.

cheesy cauliflower & broccoli bake

Preparation time **10 minutes**
Cooking time **20 minutes**
Serves 4

¼ cup **butter**
1 **cauliflower,** cut into florets
1 head of **broccoli,** cut into
   florets
2½ tablespoons **cornstarch**
1¼ cups **milk**
4 oz **Gruyère cheese,** grated
8 **streaky bacon slices,**
   cooked until crisp
1 cup **gluten-free fresh bread
   crumbs**
salt and **black pepper**

Heat half the butter in a skillet, add the cauliflower and broccoli, and fry until just tender. Transfer to an ovenproof dish.

Melt the remaining butter in a saucepan, add the cornstarch and cook, stirring, for 1 minute. Gradually add the milk and cook, stirring all the time, until thickened and smooth, then season well with salt and pepper. Stir in two-thirds of the Gruyère, then crumble in half the bacon.

Pour the sauce over the vegetables. Mix together the remaining Gruyère and the bread crumbs and sprinkle over the top with the remaining bacon.

Place in a preheated oven, 400°F, for 10–12 minutes until golden and bubbling.

For leek & Jerusalem artichoke gratin, replace the cauliflower and broccoli with 3 finely sliced large leeks and 10 oz peeled and sliced Jerusalem artichokes and cook as above until softened. Spoon into an ovenproof dish. Mix together 2 cups gluten-free fresh bread crumbs, 2 oz crumbled feta cheese, and 2 oz grated Gruyère cheese in a bowl, sprinkle over the leek mixture and press down gently. Cook in the oven as above.

rice & corn omelet

Preparation time **5 minutes**
Cooking time **10 minutes**
Serves **4**

½ oz **butter**
4 **scallions**, shredded
1 **red chili**, seeded and finely
   sliced (optional)
7 oz can **corn kernels**, drained
1½ cups cooked **long-grain**
   or **basmati rice**
handful of **fresh herbs**,
   chopped
6 **eggs**, beaten
3 tablespoons grated
   Parmesan cheese
salt and **black pepper**

Heat the butter in a large skillet, add the scallions and chili, and fry for 2 minutes. Add the corn, rice, and herbs and stir to combine.

Pour in the eggs, season well with salt and pepper, and cook for 2–3 minutes until beginning to set.

Sprinkle with the Parmesan, then place under a hot broiler and cook until firm and golden. Turn out and cut into generous wedges to serve.

For chorizo & potato omelet, heat 1 tablespoon olive oil in a skillet, add 1 sliced onion and fry for 3–4 minutes until softened. Add 4 oz chopped chorizo sausage and fry for 2 minutes more until it begins to crisp. Stir in 10 oz cooked sliced potatoes and a handful of chopped parsley. Stir to combine, then pour in the beaten eggs. Cook under a hot grill.

ricotta & spinach tart

Preparation time **15 minutes**, plus chilling
Cooking time **30 minutes**
Serves **4**

1 cup **rice flour**, plus extra for dusting
²/₃ cup **cornmeal**
½ cup **butter**, cubed
½ cup grated **Parmesan cheese**
1 **egg yolk**
2 tablespoons **milk**

Filling
1 teaspoon **olive oil**
1 **shallot**, finely chopped
1 **garlic clove**, crushed
4 cups **baby leaf spinach**
1¼ cups **ricotta cheese**
½ cup **light sour cream**
4 tablespoons grated **Parmesan cheese**
2 **eggs**, lightly beaten
grating of **nutmeg**
salt and **black pepper**

Place the flour, cornmeal, butter, and Parmesan in a food processor and whiz until the mixture resembles fine bread crumbs. Alternatively, mix together the rice flour and polenta in a bowl. Add the butter and rub in with the fingertips until the mixture resembles fine bread crumbs. Stir in the Parmesan.

Mix together the egg yolk and milk in a separate bowl and add enough to the dry ingredients to form a soft but not sticky dough. Wrap the dough in plastic wrap and chill for 30 minutes.

Roll the dough out on a surface lightly dusted with rice flour and use to line a 8 inch fluted tart pan. Prick the pastry base with a fork and place in a preheated oven, 400°F, for 10 minutes. Remove from the oven. Make the filling while the pastry is cooking. Heat the oil in a skillet and soften the shallot and garlic for 2–3 minutes. Add the spinach and cook for 3–4 minutes until wilted and any moisture has evaporated.

Beat together the ricotta, sour cream, half the Parmesan, and the eggs in a bowl, then season well with nutmeg and salt and pepper. Stir in the spinach mixture and pour into the tart case, sprinkle with the remaining Parmesan, and return to the oven for 20 minutes until firm and golden.

For creamy smoked trout tart, make and bake the tart case as above. For the filling, beat together 2 eggs, 6 tablespoons cream cheese, ¾ cup light sour cream, 1 tablespoon creamed horseradish, and 2 tablespoons snipped chives in a bowl. Fold in 5 oz sliced smoked trout, pour into the pan, and cook in the oven for 20–25 minutes until firm and golden.

vietnamese rice paper rolls

Preparation time **15 minutes**
Makes **12**

4 oz **cooked peeled shrimp**
¼ **cucumber**, cut into
   matchsticks
handful of **cilantro**, chopped
handful of **mint**, chopped
handful of **Thai basil**, chopped
5 oz cold cooked **rice noodles**
¼ **iceberg lettuce**, shredded
12 **round rice paper sheets**
lime wedges, to serve

Dipping sauce
2 tablespoons **sweet chili
   dipping sauce**
juice of 1 **lime**
1 tablespoon **Thai fish sauce**
1 tablespoon **sesame seeds**,
   toasted

Mix together the shrimp, cucumber, herbs, noodles, and lettuce in a large bowl.

Soak 1 rice sheet in a bowl of warm water for 20 seconds, then drain on paper towels. Fill with the shrimp mixture, leaving about 1 inch at the top and the bottom of the sheet. Fold over the top and bottom edges and roll up. Repeat with the remaining rice sheets and filling.

Whisk together all the dipping sauce ingredients in a serving dish and serve with the rolls and lime wedges.

For crab rolls, omit the shrimp and cucumber and replace with 7 oz fresh white crabmeat and 4 finely sliced scallions. Continue as above. Serve with chopped peanuts.

double-baked cheese soufflés

Preparation time **15 minutes**
Cooking time **30–40 minutes**
Serves **4**

2 tablespoons **butter**, plus
  extra, melted, for greasing
3 tablespoons **rice flour**
1 cup **milk**
3 oz **blue cheese**, crumbled
¾ cup grated **Parmesan
  cheese**
1 teaspoon **gluten-free
  English mustard**
1 tablespoon **snipped chives**
1 tablespoon **thyme leaves**
2 **eggs**, separated
6 tablespoons **heavy cream**
salt and **black pepper**

Brush 4 small ramekins with melted butter, to grease.

Heat the butter in a saucepan, add the flour, and cook, stirring, for 1 minute. Gradually add the milk and cook, stirring all the time, until thickened and smooth. Remove from the heat and cool a little. Stir in the blue cheese, half the Parmesan, the mustard, herbs, and egg yolks and season well.

Whisk the egg whites in a clean bowl until they form soft peaks, then gently fold into the cheese sauce. Spoon into the prepared ramekins, then place in a roasting pan. Pour boiling water into the pan to come halfway up the ramekins and then place in a preheated oven, 350°F, for 15–20 minutes until firm. Cool completely.

Mix together the cream and the remaining Parmesan when ready to serve and spoon over the soufflés. Place in a preheated oven, 425°F for 10–15 minutes or until golden and risen. Serve with a watercress salad.

For blue cheese soufflé omelet for one, separate 3 large eggs and whisk the whites in a large clean bowl until they form soft peaks. Gently fold in the egg yolks, 1 oz crumbled blue cheese, and 2 snipped scallions. Heat 1 teaspoon butter in a medium skillet, pour in the egg mixture, and cook for 1 minute. Sprinkle with 1 tablespoon grated Parmesan cheese and place under a hot broiler until golden and just set. Serve with a green salad.

suppers

vegetable & feta bake

Preparation time **10 minutes**
Cooking time **1 hour 10
  minutes**
Serves **4**

4 tablespoons **olive oil**
1 **eggplant**, halved and sliced
3 **zucchini**, sliced
1 **onion**, sliced
2 **garlic cloves**, finely sliced
1 lb 5 oz **potatoes**, scrubbed
  and cubed
1¾ cups **puréed tomatoes**
15 **cherry tomatoes**
handful of **fresh herbs**,
  chopped
7 oz **feta cheese**, crumbled
2 cups **fresh gluten-free
  wholewheat bread crumbs**
salt and **black pepper**

Heat the oil in a large flameproof dish, add the
eggplant, zucchini, onion, and garlic and fry for
4–5 minutes.

Add the potatoes, puréed tomatoes, tomatoes, and
herbs to the pan and season with salt and pepper.
Stir well, then place in a preheated oven 400°F for
45 minutes. Remove from the oven.

Sprinkle the feta and bread crumbs over the roasted
vegetable mixture, return to the oven, and continue to
cook for 12–15 minutes until golden.

For vegetable & shrimp bake, make as above and
cook for 45 minutes in the oven. Stir in 10 oz raw
peeled jumbo shrimp, then sprinkle with the feta and
bread crumbs and continue to cook as above.

teriyaki beef with rice noodles

Preparation time **15 minutes**, plus marinating
Cooking time **10 minutes**
Serves **4**

1 lb **sirloin steak**
10 oz **dried rice ribbon noodles**
2 teaspoons **sesame oil**
1 tablespoon peeled and grated **fresh ginger root**
1 **garlic clove**, finely sliced
1 cup sliced **snow peas**
1 **carrot,** cut into matchsticks
4 **scallions**, shredded
handful of **cilantro**, chopped

Teriyaki marinade
2 tablespoons **gluten-free soy sauce**
2 tablespoons **sake**
1 tablespoon **mirin**
½ tablespoon **superfine sugar**

Make the marinade by mixing together all the ingredients in a small jug. Place the beef in a dish, pour over the marinade, cover, and marinate in the refrigerator for at least 2 hours, preferably overnight.

Soak the rice noodles in boiling water according to the package instructions.

Drain well. Meanwhile, preheat a griddle so that it is really hot. Place the beef on the griddle, reserving the marinade, and cook for 2–3 minutes on each side. Transfer to a cutting board and allow to rest.

Heat the oil in a wok or large skillet, add the ginger and garlic, and fry for 30 seconds. Add the vegetables and cook until just beginning to soften.

Add the cilantro, noodles, and 2–3 tablespoons of the marinade and heat through. Spoon onto 4 serving plates, slice the beef, and serve on top of the noodles.

For Thai beef salad, mix together the marinade ingredients as above, adding 1 teaspoon sesame oil, the grated zest and juice of 1 lime, 3 tablespoons Thai fish sauce, a handful each of cilantro, mint, and chopped Thai basil. Cover and chill. When ready to serve, griddle the beef as above. Using a peeler, slice ½ cucumber and 2 carrots into ribbons and stir into the chilled dressing with 4 shredded scallions, 12 halved cherry tomatoes, and 4 cups salad leaves. Slice the steak thinly, stir into the salad, and serve.

chicken in a pot

Preparation time **10 minutes**
Cooking time **1 hour 30 minutes**
Serves **4**

2 tablespoons **olive oil**
4 oz **bacon**, chopped
2 **onions**, cut into wedges
1 lb **baby carrots**, halved
1¼ lb **new potatoes**, halved if large
1 **garlic bulb**, halved across the middle
bunch of **thyme**
1 **fennel bulb**, sliced
3 lb **whole chicken**
2 large glasses **dry white wine**
salt and **black pepper**

Heat the oil in a large flameproof casserole, add the bacon and fry for 1–2 minutes until beginning to brown. Add all the remaining ingredients and season well with salt and pepper.

Cover and place in a preheated oven, 400°F, for 1 hour.

Remove the lid and cook for 30 minutes more or until the juices run clear when the thickest part of the leg is pierced with a knife. Serve with large hunks of crusty gluten-free bread, if liked.

For braised peas, to serve as an accompaniment, heat 2 tablespoons butter and 1 tablespoon olive oil in a large skillet, add 4 oz chopped bacon or pancetta and fry for 2 minutes or until beginning to crisp. Add 2 cups fresh or frozen peas and 6 tablespoons gluten-free chicken stock and cook for 3–4 minutes. Stir in 1 tablespoon chopped mint and the juice of ½ lemon and season well with salt and pepper.

roasted butternut squash risotto

Preparation time **10 minutes**
Cooking time **25 minutes**
Serves **4**

1 **butternut squash**, peeled,
   seeded, and cut into
   1 inch cubes
3 tablespoons **olive oil**
handful of **sage leaves**
1 **onion**, chopped
1 cup **risotto rice**
1 glass **dry white wine**
2½ cups **gluten-free**
   vegetable stock
4 tablespoons grated
   Parmesan cheese
½ oz **butter**
3 oz **blue cheese**, crumbled
2 cups **arugula leaves**
salt and **black pepper**

Put the squash on a baking sheet, drizzle over half the oil, and sprinkle with the sage leaves. Place in a preheated oven, 400°F, and cook for 20–25 minutes until golden and tender.

Heat the remaining oil in a large skillet, while the squash is roasting. Add the onion and fry for 3–4 minutes until softened, then mix in the rice and coat with the oil. Pour in the wine and cook, stirring, until the liquid is absorbed.

Add the stock a ladleful at a time, stirring continually, adding the next ladle only once the previous one has been absorbed. When the rice is al dente, remove the pan from the heat, stir in the Parmesan and butter and season well with salt and pepper.

Top the risotto with the squash and serve in shallow bowls with the blue cheese and arugula scattered over.

For wild mushroom risotto, place 5 tablespoons dried porcini mushrooms in a bowl and pour over boiling water to just cover. Soak for 5 minutes, then chop the mushrooms and strain the soaking liquid. Omit the squash and cook the risotto as above, adding the mushrooms and liquid with the last addition of stock. Once the rice is al dente, stir in a handful of chopped parsley and serve.

polenta mini pizzas

Preparation time **10 minutes**
Cooking time **20 minutes**
Makes **10**

2½ cups **gluten-free
vegetable stock**
1 cup **instant cornmeal**
¼ cup grated **Parmesan
cheese**

Topping
2 large **tomatoes**, sliced
3 oz **prosciutto**, roughly torn
5 oz **Gorgonzola cheese**,
crumbled
⅓ cup **pine nuts**, toasted
1 tablespoon **olive oil**, plus
extra for oiling
handful of basil leaves

Put the stock in a saucepan and bring to a boil, then stir in the cornmeal and Parmesan over a low heat. Continue to cook, stirring, until thick.

Turn out onto a lightly oiled surface and spread out to a thickness of ½ inch. Using a plain cutter, stamp out 10 rounds a little larger than the tomato slices and place on a lightly oiled baking sheet.

Top each 'pizza' with a slice of tomato, some prosciutto, Gorgonzola, and pine nuts and drizzle over a little oil.

Place in a preheated oven, 425°F, for 10–12 minutes until golden. Sprinkle with the basil leaves and serve.

For tomato, spinach, & mozzarella pizzas, make the cornmeal pizza bases as above. Replace the large tomatoes with 12 chopped cherry tomatoes and sprinkle over the pizzas with 3 tablespoons cooked and well-squeezed chopped baby leaf spinach and 5 oz torn mozzarella cheese. Drizzle with a little olive oil and sprinkle with the basil. Cook in the oven as above.

chicken tagine

Preparation time **20 minutes**, plus marinating

Cooking time **1 hour 40 minutes**

Serves **4**

8 large skinless **chicken thighs** on the bone, or 1 **whole chicken**, jointed
1 teaspoon **ground cumin**
1 teaspoon **ground cilantro**
½ teaspoon **ground turmeric**
1 teaspoon **ground ginger**
1 teaspoon **paprika**
3 tablespoons **olive oil**
2 **onions**, cut into wedges
2 **garlic cloves**, finely sliced
1 **fennel bulb**, sliced
10 oz small **new potatoes**
handful of **golden raisins**
8 **ready-to-eat dried apricots**
½ cup **green olives** (optional)
pinch of **saffron threads**
1¾ cups hot **gluten-free chicken stock**
small bunch of **cilantro**, chopped
salt and **black pepper**

Slash each piece of chicken 2–3 times with a small knife. Mix together the spices and half the olive oil, rub over the chicken pieces, cover, and marinate in the refrigerator for at least 2 hours, preferably overnight.

Heat the remaining oil in a tagine or large flameproof casserole, add the chicken pieces and fry for 4–5 minutes until golden all over. Add the onion, garlic, and fennel to the pan and continue to fry for 2–3 minutes.

Add all the remaining ingredients, except the cilantro, and stir well. Cover and simmer for about 1½ hours or until the chicken begins to fall off the bone. Season well and stir in the cilantro.

For lamb tagine with prunes & almonds, marinate 1¼ lb cubed lean lamb in the spice and olive oil mixture, then continue with the recipe as above but replace the apricots with 8 prunes. Cover and simmer for about 2 hours or until the meat is cooked through and tender. Stir in a handful of toasted slivered almonds with the cilantro before serving.

crusted salmon with tomato salsa

Preparation time **10 minutes**
Cooking time **12–15 minutes**
Serves **4**

1 tablespoon chopped
  fresh herbs
1 **garlic clove**, crushed
3 tablespoons **cornmeal**
4 pieces of **skinless salmon
  fillet**, about 4 oz each
black pepper
4 tablespoons **light sour
  cream**, to serve
green salad, to serve

Salsa
20 **cherry tomatoes**,
  quartered
1 small **red onion**, finely sliced
½ **red chili**, seeded and finely
  chopped
handful of **cilantro**, chopped

Mix together the herbs, garlic, and cornmeal in a shallow bowl. Coat the salmon pieces in the cornmeal mix, pressing it down firmly.

Put the coated fish on a baking sheet and place in a preheated oven, 400°F, for 12–15 minutes until cooked through.

Mix together the salsa ingredients in a bowl. Place the salmon on 4 serving plates, top with the salsa and a spoonful of sour cream, season with black pepper and serve with a green salad.

For cornmeal-crusted chicken, beat together 2 tablespoons cream cheese with the chopped fresh herbs and 1 peeled, chopped garlic clove. Make a horizontal slit in each of 4 boneless, skinless chicken breasts. Fill the cavities of the chicken breasts with the cream cheese mixture, then secure with toothpicks. Dip the chicken breasts in a little gluten-free flour, a little beaten egg, then in the cornmeal. Fry in olive oil for 2–3 minutes on each side, transfer to a baking sheet and place in a preheated oven, 400°F, for 10–12 minutes or until the chicken is cooked through. Serve with the salsa and a green salad.

lamb kofte with tzatziki & salad

Preparation time **15 minutes**
Cooking time **6–7 minutes**
Serves **4**

1 lb **ground lamb**
2 teaspoons **ground cumin**
2 teaspoons **thyme leaves**
1 teaspoon **chili powder**
grated zest of ½ **lemon**
salt and **black pepper**

Tzatziki
¾ cup whole milk **Greek yogurt**
¼ **cucumber**, grated
handful of **mint**, chopped
juice of ½ **lemon**
1 **garlic clove**, crushed

Red onion salad
1 large **red onion**, finely sliced
2 large **tomatoes**, thinly sliced
2 tablespoons **olive oil**
1 tablespoon **red wine vinegar**

Mix together the lamb, cumin, thyme, chili powder, and lemon zest in a bowl and season well with salt and pepper. Divide the mixture into 8 and shape around 8 metal skewers.

Place the skewers under a hot broiler or on the barbecue for about 6–7 minutes, turning occasionally, until golden and cooked through.

Combine all the tzatziki ingredients in a serving dish. Mix together all the salad ingredients in a serving bowl.

Serve the kofte with the tzatziki, red onion salad, and toasted gluten-free bread or steamed rice, if desired.

For spiced chicken skewers, whisk together the grated zest and juice of 1 orange, 1 teaspoon peeled and grated fresh ginger root, 1 tablespoon gluten-free soy sauce, 1 tablespoon sesame oil, 1 tablespoon honey, and 1 teaspoon dried chili flakes in a nonmetallic bowl. Stir in 3 cubed boneless, skinless chicken breasts and marinate in the refrigerator for at least 20 minutes. Thread the chicken onto skewers with red onion wedges and chunks of red bell pepper. Place under a hot broiler or on the barbecue for 5–6 minutes, or until beginning to char and cooked through.

chicken & leek gratin

Preparation time **15 minutes**
Cooking time **40–45 minutes**
Serves **4**

1 tablespoon **olive oil**
1 **onion**, chopped
1 **garlic clove**, crushed
4 **leeks**, trimmed, cleaned,
  and chopped
4 **boneless, skinless chicken
  breasts**, cut into chunks
1 small glass **dry white wine**
1 tablespoon **rice flour**
1¼ cups **gluten-free chicken
  stock**
²/₃ cup **heavy cream**
2 tablespoons chopped
  tarragon
1 tablespoon **gluten-free
  English mustard**
4 cups **fresh gluten-free
  bread crumbs**
4 oz **Gruyère cheese**, grated
salt and **black pepper**

Heat the oil in a large saucepan, add the onion, garlic, and leeks and fry for 3–4 minutes. Transfer the vegetables to a plate, add the chicken to the pan, and fry for 3 minutes until beginning to brown all over.

Add the wine and simmer until it has reduced by about half. Add the flour and cook, stirring, for 1 minute, then gradually add the stock and cook, stirring all the time, until the sauce has thickened.

Stir in the leek mixture, cream, tarragon and mustard and season well with salt and pepper. Transfer to an ovenproof dish, then sprinkle with the bread crumbs and Gruyère.

Place in a preheated oven, 400°F, for 25–30 minutes until golden and bubbling. Serve with steamed vegetables.

For chicken & mushroom pasta bake, cook 12 oz gluten-free pasta shapes in a saucepan of boiling water according to the package instructions, then drain well. Meanwhile, fry the onion and garlic as above, with 1 lb mixed sliced mushrooms. Continue as above, stirring the mushroom mixture into the sauce with the cream, tarragon, and mustard. Season well and add the pasta, then transfer to an ovenproof dish, sprinkle over the bread crumbs and Gruyere and bake as above.

seafood noodles

Preparation time **10 minutes**
Cooking time **7–10 minutes**
Serves **4**

12 oz **dried rice noodles**
3 tablespoons **olive oil**
1 small **onion**, finely chopped
3 **garlic cloves**, crushed
2 inches **fresh ginger**, peeled
and finely grated
1 **red chili**, seeded and finely
chopped
12 **cherry tomatoes**,
quartered
1 lb **raw jumbo shrimp**,
peeled and deveined
7 oz **fresh white crabmeat**
3 tablespoons chopped
parsley

Soak the noodles in boiling water according to the package instructions. Drain well.

Heat the oil in a large skillet, add the onion, garlic, ginger, and chili and fry for 1–2 minutes until softened.

Add the tomatoes and shrimp and cook for 2–3 minutes, or until the shrimp are cooked through and piping hot.

Stir in the crabmeat and parsley, combine with the noodles, and serve immediately.

For hearty seafood laksa, cook the onion, garlic, ginger, and chili as above. Process ½ teaspoon turmeric and the inner stems of 2 lemon grass stalks in a small food processor or blender to a paste. Gently fry the lemon grass paste with the onion mixture for 2 minutes, then add 1¾ cups coconut milk and 4 cups gluten-free fish or vegetable stock and simmer for 10 minutes. Stir in 1 lb cooked peeled and deveined jumbo shrimp, 7 oz fresh white crabmeat, 2 tablespoons chopped cilantro, and 8 oz soaked rice noodles. Heat through and serve.

fruity stuffed peppers

Preparation time **15 minutes**
Cooking time **1 hour**
Serves **4**

2 **red bell peppers**, cored,
   seeded, and halved
2 **orange peppers**, cored,
   seeded, and halved
2 tablespoons **olive oil**, plus
   extra for brushing
1 **red onion**, chopped
1 **garlic clove**, crushed
1 small **red chili**, seeded and
   finely chopped
3 tablespoons **pine nuts**
1½ cups cooked **wild rice**
13 oz can **green lentils**,
   drained and rinsed
12 **cherry tomatoes**,
   quartered
²/₃ cup **ready-to-eat dried
   apricots**, chopped
handful of **golden raisins**
grated zest of 1 **lemon**
2 tablespoons chopped **fresh
   herbs**
4 oz **feta cheese**, crumbled

Put the peppers in an ovenproof dish, cut side up, and brush each with a little oil. Place in a preheated oven, 400°F, for 20 minutes.

Heat the oil in skillet, add the onion, garlic, and chili and fry for 2 minutes, then add the pine nuts and cook for 2 minutes more until golden. Stir in all the remaining ingredients.

Remove the peppers from the oven and spoon the stuffing mixture into the peppers. Cover with foil, return to the oven, and cook for 25 minutes, then remove the foil and cook for an additional 15 minutes. Serve with a crisp salad.

For fruity stuffed eggplants, roughly prick 2 large eggplants all over with a fork. Place on a baking sheet and place in a preheated oven, 400°F, for 30 minutes. Remove from the oven and halve lengthways, scoop out most of the flesh, and roughly chop. Make the stuffing as above, adding the eggplant flesh to the pan with the onion, garlic, and chili. Spoon the mixture into the eggplant skins and cook as above.

bacon & spinach pasta

Preparation time **10 minutes**
Cooking time **15 minutes**
Serves **4**

12 oz **gluten-free pasta**
1 tablespoon **olive oil**
7 oz **bacon**, sliced
1 **onion**, sliced
2 tablespoons **pine nuts**
3½ cups **baby leaf spinach**
20 **cherry tomatoes**, halved
6 tablespoons **light cream**
2 tablespoons grated
　Parmesan cheese
4 **scallions**, sliced
salt and **black pepper**

Cook the pasta in a saucepan of salted boiling water according to the package instructions. Drain well.

Heat the oil in a skillet, add the bacon and onion, and fry for 3–4 minutes until the bacon is crisp and the onion softened.

Add the pine nuts and cook for 1 minute. Stir in the spinach and tomatoes and cook until the spinach is just wilted.

Stir the spinach mixture into the pasta. Mix in the cream, Parmesan, and scallions, season well with salt and pepper, and serve immediately.

For broccoli, bacon, & blue cheese pasta, cook the pasta as above, adding 10 oz broccoli florets 4 minutes before the end of cooking time. Drain well. Meanwhile, fry the bacon as above, omitting the onion. Stir in 2/3 cup light cream and 4 oz crumbled blue cheese. Mix into the pasta and broccoli and serve immediately.

thai coconut chicken

Preparation time **20 minutes**
Cooking time **40–45 minutes**
Serves **4**

2 cups **gluten-free chicken
   stock**
4 **boneless, skinless chicken
   breasts**, cubed
1 tablespoon **peanut oil**
1¾ cups **coconut milk**
salt and **black pepper**
roughly chopped **cilantro**, to
   garnish
cooked rice ribbon noodles,
   or **fragrant rice**, to serve

Curry paste
1 **green chili**, seeded and
   roughly chopped
1 small **onion**, roughly
   chopped
3 **garlic cloves**, chopped
2 oz **cilantro**
2 teaspoons **Thai fish sauce**
¼ teaspoon **ground turmeric**
1 **lemon grass stalk**, roughly
   chopped
grated zest and juice of 1 **lime**
2 teaspoons **superfine sugar**
1 tablespoon roughly chopped
   fresh ginger root

Make the curry paste. Put all the paste ingredients
in a food processor or blender and blitz until smooth,
scraping the mixture down from the side of the bowl
if necessary.

Put the stock and curry paste in a large saucepan and
bring to the boil. Cook, uncovered, for 15–20 minutes
until most of the liquid has evaporated.

Season the chicken lightly with salt and pepper. Heat
the oil in a large skillet, add the chicken, and gently fry
for 5 minutes.

Add the chicken and coconut milk to the reduced curry
sauce and cook for about 20 minutes until the chicken
is very tender. Ladle into shallow bowls, sprinkle with
cilantro, and serve with fragrant rice or rice noodles.

For Thai coconut tofu, make the curry paste as above,
replacing the fish sauce with 2 teaspoons gluten-free
soy sauce. Continue as above, replacing the chicken
stock with 2 cups gluten-free vegetable stock and the
chicken with 7 oz cubed firm tofu.

harissa salmon with sweet potato

Preparation time **10 minutes,
plus marinating**
Cooking time **35–40 minutes**
Serves **4**

2 tablespoons **plain yogurt**
2 teaspoons **harissa**
2 tablespoons chopped
   cilantro, plus extra to garnish
grated zest and juice of
   ½ **lime**
4 pieces of **skinless salmon
   fillet**, about 5 oz each
vegetable oil, for oiling
lime wedges, to serve

Spicy sweet potato
1 lb **sweet potato**, peeled and
   cut into chunks
1 tablespoon **olive oil**
1 teaspoon **cumin seeds**
½ teaspoon **garam masala**
salt and **black pepper**

Mix together the yogurt, harissa, cilantro, and lime zest and juice in a nonmetallic bowl. Add the salmon and coat in the mixture. Cover and marinate in the refrigerator for at least 20 minutes.

Toss together the sweet potato chunks, olive oil, cumin seeds, and garam masala in a bowl and season well withh salt and pepper. Put in a roasting pan and place in a preheated oven, 400°F, for 35–40 minutes until golden.

Heat a lightly oiled skillet or griddle until hot towards the end of the sweet potato roasting time. Add the salmon and cook for 3 minutes on each side, until just cooked. Garnish with cilantro and serve with the sweet potato, lime wedges, and flat-leaf parsley.

For spiced chicken drumsticks, make the yogurt and harissa marinade as above and stir in 1 teaspoon peanut oil. Pierce the flesh of 8 skinless chicken drumsticks several times, then cover with the marinade. Marinate as above, then place under a hot broiler or on a barbecue for 12–15 minutes until cooked through and beginning to char. Serve with a salad.

loin of pork with lentils

Preparation time **15 minutes**
Cooking time about **1 hour
55 minutes**, plus resting
Serves **5–6**

1 cup **Puy lentils**
1¾ lb **pork loin**, rind removed,
   boned, and rolled
2 tablespoons **olive oil**
2 large **onions**, sliced
3 **garlic cloves**, sliced
1 tablespoon finely chopped
   rosemary
1¼ cups **gluten-free chicken**
   or **vegetable stock**
8 oz **baby carrots**, scrubbed
   and left whole
salt and **black pepper**

Put the lentils in a saucepan, cover with water, and bring to a boil. Boil rapidly for 10 minutes, then drain well.

Sprinkle the pork with salt and pepper. Heat the oil in a large heavy skillet and brown the meat on all sides. Transfer to a casserole dish and add the lentils.

Add the onions to the pan and fry for 5 minutes. Stir in the garlic, rosemary, and stock and bring to a boil. Pour over the meat and lentils and cover with a lid. Place in a preheated oven, 350°F, for 1 hour.

Stir the carrots into the casserole, season well with salt and pepper, and return to the oven for 20–30 minutes more until the pork is cooked through and the lentils are soft. Drain the meat, transfer to a serving platter, and allow to rest in a warm place for 20 minutes. Carve into thin slices, then serve with the lentils, carrots, and juices.

For apricot stuffed pork, heat 1 tablespoon olive oil in a skillet, add 1 chopped onion and 1 crushed garlic clove and fry for 3–4 minutes until softened. Stir in ²/₃ cup finely chopped ready-to-eat dried apricots, 2 tablespoons pine nuts, 1 tablespoon chopped sage, and 2 tablespoons fresh gluten-free bread crumbs. Remove from the heat, stir to combine, then spread inside the pork before rolling up and frying at intervals along its lenght with kitchen string. Follow the recipe above, but cook the stuffed pork with the lentils in the oven for about 1¼ hours before adding the carrots and cooking for a further 20–30 minutes as above.

wild rice & griddled chicken salad

Preparation time **10 minutes**,
  plus marinating
Cooking time **35 minutes**
Serves **4**

1 **garlic clove**, crushed
2 teaspoons **olive oil**
1 teaspoon **balsamic vinegar**
4 small **boneless, skinless
  chicken breasts**, halved
  horizontally

Rice salad
1 cup mixed **wild** and
  basmati rice
2 **red bell peppers**, roasted,
  cored, seeded, and sliced
3 **scallions**, sliced
8 **cherry tomatoes**, quartered
2 cups **arugula leaves**
3 oz **soft goat cheese**,
  crumbled

Dressing
juice of ½ **lemon**
1 teaspoon **gluten-free
  Dijon mustard**
1 teaspoon **honey**
2 tablespoons **olive oil**

Mix together the garlic, olive oil, and vinegar in
a nonmetallic bowl, add the chicken and coat in
the marinade. Cover and leave to marinate in the
refrigerator for at least 30 minutes.

Cook the rice in a saucepan of boiling water according
to the package instructions. Drain well and leave to cool,
then mix with the peppers, scallions, tomatoes, argula,
and goat cheese in a large bowl.

Whisk together the dressing ingredients in a bowl
and stir into the rice salad. Spoon the salad onto 4
serving plates.

Heat a griddle pan until hot and cook the chicken
for 3–4 minutes on each side until cooked through.
Immediately before serving, slice the griddled chicken
and arrange on top of the salad.

For wild rice, orange, & haloumi salad, make the
rice salad as above, replacing the red peppers with
the sliced flesh of 2 oranges. and omitting the goats'
cheese. Make the dressing as above and stir into the
salad. Cut 7 oz haloumi cheese into slices, brush with
a little olive oil, and season with plenty of black pepper.
Heat a griddle pan until hot and cook the haloumi for
1–2 minutes on each side until browned. Arrange on
top of the rice salad and serve.

spinach & fish pie

Preparation time **15 minutes**
Cooking time **45–55 minutes**
Serves **4**

7 oz **raw shrimp**, peeled and
   deveined
1 tablespoon **olive oil**
1 **onion**, chopped
3½ cups **baby leaf spinach**
¼ cup **butter**
3 tablespoons **rice flour**
2½ cups **milk**
1 tablespoon **gluten-free**
   whole grain mustard
good grating of **nutmeg**
1 lb 5 oz mixed **skinless**
   salmon, haddock, and
   smoked haddock fillets, cut
   into chunks
salt and **black pepper**

Potato topping
2 lb **potatoes**, peeled and cut
   into chunks
good knob of **butter**
6 tablespoons **light cream**

Make the potato topping. Cook the potatoes in a
saucepan of salted boiling water for 15 minutes or until
tender. Drain well and return to the pan. Mash together
with the butter and cream and season well with salt
and pepper.

Heat the oil in a large saucepan, add the onion, and
fry for 2–3 minutes until beginning to soften. Add the
spinach to the pan and cook until wilted and any liquid
has evaporated.

Melt the butter in a saucepan, add the flour and cook,
stirring, for 1 minute. Gradually add the milk and cook,
stirring all the time, until thickened and smooth. Stir in
the mustard and nutmeg and season well.

Arrange the fish and the shrimp in a large ovenproof
dish. Pour the sauce over the fish, spoon the mash on
top and place in a preheated oven, 400°F, for 30–35
minutes until golden and bubbling.

For rosti-topped fish pie, steam 3 peeled baking
potatoes for 12–15 minutes, then grate into a large
bowl. Stir in 2 tablespoons melted butter and season
well with salt and pepper. Make the sauce as above and
pour over the fish and shrimp in a large overproof dish.
Spread the rosti over the fish and sauce and cook
as above.

chili rice noodles

Preparation time **10 minutes**
Cooking time **7–10 minutes**
Serves **4**

8 teaspoons **seasoned rice vinegar**

2 tablespoons **superfine sugar**

2 teaspoons **Thai fish sauce**

2 tablespoons **gluten-free soy sauce**

7 oz **dried rice ribbon noodles**

2 tablespoons **vegetable** or **peanut oil**

1 **red chili**, seeded and finely shredded

1 large **red bell pepper**, cored, seeded, and finely shredded

1 cup **snow peas**, thinly sliced lengthwise

Mix together the vinegar, sugar, fish sauce, and soy sauce in a bowl. Put the noodles in another bowl and cover with boiling water. Leave for 3–4 minutes until soft.

Heat the oil in a skillet, while the noodles are soaking, add the chilli, red pepper, and snow peas and fry for 4–5 minutes until softened.

Drain the noodles and add to the pan with the vinegar mixture. Toss together and serve immediately.

For chili chicken & baby corn noodles, mix together the vinegar, sugar, fish sauce, and soy sauce and cook the noodles as above. Heat the oil in a skillet, add 3 sliced boneless, skinless chicken breasts and fry for 2–3 minutes until beginning to brown. Add the chili, red pepper, snow peas, and 14 oz baby corn and fry for 3 minutes more. Combine with the drained noodles and vinegar mixture as above.

spring lamb stew & dumplings

Preparation time **15 minutes**

Cooking time **1 hour 45 minutes**

Serves **4**

2 tablespoons **gluten-free all-purpose flour**

1½ lb **lean lamb**, cubed

2 tablespoons **olive oil**

12 **shallots**, peeled

2 **garlic cloves**, sliced

1 tablespoon **tomato paste**

thyme sprig

1 **bay leaf**

1¼ cups **red wine**

2½ cups **gluten-free chicken stock**

1½ lb cooked **baby carrots,** peeled and chopped **turnips,** and **new potatoes**

2 cups **green beans**, topped and tailed

salt and **black pepper**

Dumplings

1 cup **rice flour**

1 teaspoon **gluten-free baking powder**

½ cup **gluten-free suet**

handful of **fresh herbs**, chopped

Season the flour well, then toss the lamb in the flour. Heat the oil in a large flameproof casserole, add the meat in batches, and fry until browned all over.

Add the shallots and garlic and fry for 1 minute, then stir in the tomato paste, thyme, and bay leaf.

Stir in the red wine and stock gradually, bring to a gentle simmer, then cover and cook for 1 hour or until the meat is almost tender.

Make the dumplings. Mix together all the ingredients in a large bowl, season, and then add enough cold water to make a soft dough. Shape into 12 balls.

Stir the vegetables into the stew, then top with the dumplings. Cover and continue to cook for 25–30 minutes until the vegetables are tender.

For sweet potato & eggplant stew, omit the lamb and fry the shallots and garlic with 2 large peeled and cubed sweet potatoes and 1 chopped eggplant for 4–5 minutes until beginning to soften. Continue as above, replacing the chicken stock with a 2½ cups gluten-free vegetable stock. Gently simmer for 20 minutes, then add 1½ cups green beans just before topping with the dumplings. Cover and cook for a further 25–30 minutes.

spiced haddock & cumin potatoes

Preparation time **10 minutes**,
   plus marinating
Cooking time **40 minutes**
Serves **4**

4 pieces of **haddock fillet**,
   about 5 oz each

Spice rub
½ teaspoon **paprika**
1 teaspoon **ground cumin**
1 **garlic clove**, crushed
2 inches **fresh ginger root**,
   peeled and finely grated
½ teaspoon **ground cilantro**
1 tablespoon chopped
   cilantro
½ teaspoon **turmeric**
1 tablespoon **olive oil**

Cumin potatoes
1 lb **potatoes**, peeled and cut
   into chunks
1 teaspoon **cumin seeds**
1 **garlic bulb**, broken up into
   cloves
1 tablespoon **olive oil**
salt and **black pepper**

Place the fish in a dish. Mix together all the spice rub
ingredients in a bowl and rub into the fish. Cover and
marinate in the refrigerator for 30 minutes.

Mix all the cumin potato ingredients together and put
on a baking sheet. Place in a preheated oven, 400°F,
for about 40 minutes or until crisp and golden.

Heat a griddle or a skillet, meanwhile, until hot and
cook the fish for 2 minutes on each side until crisp and
golden. Serve with the potatoes and a mixed salad.

For homemade coleslaw, to serve as an
accompaniment, grate 3 peeled carrots into a large
bowl. Finely shred 1 small white or red cabbage and
stir into the carrots with 1 small sliced onion. Whisk
together 4 tablespoons light sour cream, 1 tablespoon
chopped cilantro, 1 teaspoon cumin seeds, and the
grated zest and juice of ½ lemon in a bowl and stir into
the coleslaw.

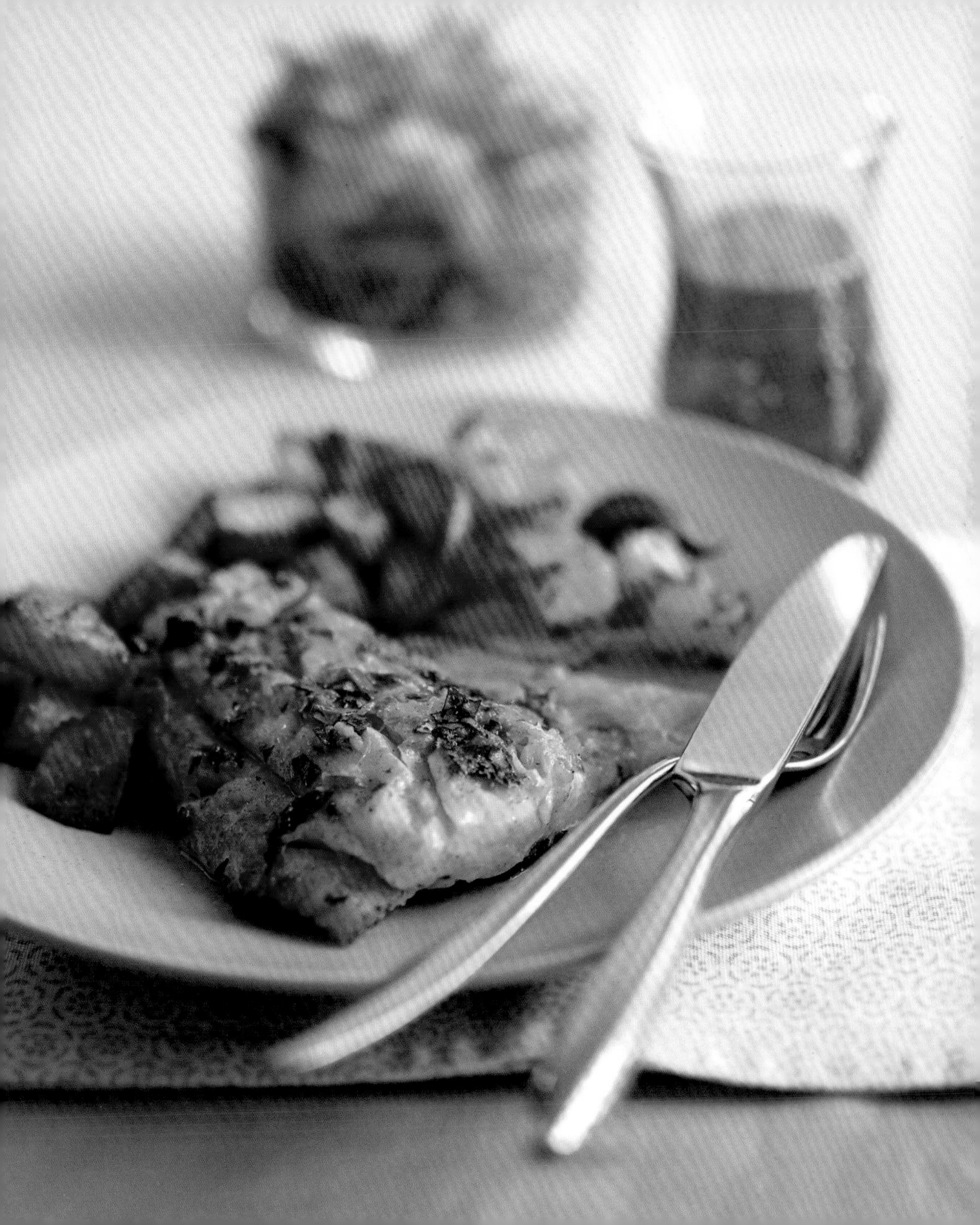

pancetta risotto with chicken

Preparation time **10 minutes**
Cooking time **25 minutes**
Serves **4**

1 tablespoon **olive oil**, plus
    extra for drizzling
5 oz **pancetta**, sliced or cubed
1 small **onion**, finely chopped
1 **garlic clove**, chopped
1½ cups **risotto rice**
½ cup **dry white wine**
3¾ cups **gluten-free chicken
    stock**
⅔ cup **petits pois**
1 teaspoon **thyme leaves**
4 small **boneless, skinless
    chicken breasts**, halved
    horizontally
2 tablespoons grated
    Parmesan cheese
salt and **black pepper**

Heat the oil in a large skillet, add the pancetta, and fry for 2 minutes until beginning to brown. Stir in the onion and garlic and continue to fry for 1–2 minutes until softened.

Mix in the rice and coat with the oil. Pour in the wine and stir until the liquid is absorbed.

Add the stock a ladleful at a time, stirring continually, adding the next ladle only once the previous one has been absorbed. With the last addition of stock, stir in the peas and thyme.

Heat a griddle until hot when almost ready to serve. Drizzle a little olive oil over the chicken and cook for 2–3 minutes on each side until cooked through. Slice the chicken then stir the Parmesan into the risotto when the rice is al dente and the peas are tender. Ladle into shallow bowls and top with the chicken. Season well.

For risotto cakes, make the risotto as above, then leave to cool completely. Once cooled, stir in 1 small egg or 1 large egg yolk and form the mixture into 8 'cakes.' Roll each risotto cake in fresh gluten-free bread crumbs, then fry in oil for 2 minutes on each side or until golden and heated through. Serve with salad.

eggplant bake

Preparation time **10 minutes**
Cooking time **40–45 minutes**
Serves **4**

2 large **eggplants**, sliced
2 tablespoons **olive oil**
5 oz **mozzarella cheese**,
   roughly chopped
4 tablespoons grated
   Parmesan cheese
salt and **black pepper**

Tomato sauce
1 tablespoon **olive oil**
1 **garlic clove**, crushed
1 small **onion**, finely chopped
13 oz can **plum tomatoes**
handful of **basil**, torn

Make the tomato sauce. Heat the oil in a saucepan, add the garlic and onion, and fry for 3–4 minutes until softened. Add the tomatoes and basil, bring to a boil and simmer for 15 minutes.

Brush the eggplants with a little oil on each side while the sauce is simmering. Heat a griddle until hot and cook the eggplant slices for 1–2 minutes on each side until tender and browned.

Spoon a little of the tomato sauce into an ovenproof dish, layer over half the eggplants, sprinkle with half the mozzarella and Parmesan and season well with salt and pepper. Repeat the layering with the remaining ingredients, finishing with a sprinkling of the cheeses.

Place in a preheated oven, 400°F, for 20–25 minutes until golden and bubbling. Serve with salad and crusty bread.

For eggplant, chili, & chicken bake, make the tomato sauce as above, adding 1 seeded and finely sliced red chili with the garlic and onion. Cook the eggplant and layer the bake as above, interspersing 10 oz shredded cooked chicken between the eggplant layers. Cook in the oven as above.

fish cakes & fennel mayonnaise

Preparation time **20 minutes**
Cooking time **25–30 minutes**
Serves **4**

1 lb **skinless cod** or
   haddock fillets
4 tablespoons **milk**
1½ lb **baking potatoes**,
   peeled and cut into chunks
2 tablespoons **butter**
2 tablespoons **capers**, rinsed
   and chopped
1 **egg**, beaten
½ cup **cornmeal**
sunflower or **olive oil**,
   for frying
salt and **black pepper**
large bunch of watercress,
   to serve

Fennel mayonnaise
6 tablespoons **mayonnaise**
3 tablespoons **plain yogurt**
3 tablespoons chopped **fennel**
2 teaspoons **hot horseradish
   sauce**

Cut the fish into chunky pieces and put in a skillet with the milk and a little seasoning. Cover and cook gently for 5 minutes until just cooked through. Drain, reserving the cooking juices.

Cook the potatoes in a saucepan of salted boiling water for 15 minutes or until tender. Drain well, tip into a bowl, and mash with a fork into chunky pieces.

Add the butter, capers, fish, and 2 tablespoons of the reserved cooking juices, and season well with salt and pepper. Mix together until the ingredients are combined but the fish and potatoes are still chunky. Shape the mixture into 8–10 balls and flatten into cakes.

Put the egg on a plate and sprinkle the cornmeal onto another plate. Coat the fish cakes first in the egg and then in the cornmeal.

Mix together the fennel mayonnaise ingredients in a serving dish. Heat ½ inch of oil in a large skillet and fry the fish cakes, in batches if necessary, for about 2 minutes on each side until golden.

Serve the mayonnaise with the hot fish cakes and a little watercress on the side.

For salmon fishcakes & cilantro mayonnaise, make as above, replacing the white fish with 1 lb skinless salmon fillets and adding the grated zest of 1 lime to the mixture. Mix the mayonnaise and yogurt with 3 tablespoons of finely chopped cilantro and a squeeze of lime juice. Fry the fish cakes as above and serve with the cilantro mayonnaise.

potato pizza margherita

Preparation time **20 minutes, plus cooling**
Cooking time **45 minutes**
Serves **3–4**

2 lb **baking potatoes**, peeled and cut into small chunks
3 tablespoons **olive oil**, plus extra for **oiling**
1 **egg**, beaten
½ cup **Parmesan** or **cheddar cheese**, grated
4 tablespoons **sundried tomato paste** or **tomato ketchup**
1 lb **small tomatoes**, thinly sliced
4 oz **mozzarella cheese**, thinly sliced
1 tablespoon chopped **thyme**, plus extra sprigs to garnish (optional)
salt

Cook the potatoes in a saucepan of salted boiling water for 15 minutes or until tender. Drain well, return to the pan, and let cool for 10 minutes.

Add 2 tablespoons of the oil, the egg, and half the grated Parmesan to the potato and mix well. Turn out onto an oiled baking sheet and spread out to form a 10 inch round. Place in a preheated oven, 400°F, for 15 minutes.

Remove from the oven and spread with the tomato paste or ketchup. Arrange the tomato and mozzarella slices on top. Sprinkle with the remaining grated Parmesan, thyme, if using, and a little salt. Drizzle with the remaining oil.

Return to the oven for an additional 15 minutes until the potato is crisp around the edges and the cheese is melting. Cut into generous wedges, garnish with thyme sprigs, if liked, and serve.

For corn & salami pizza, make as above, adding a 7 oz can drained corn kernels and 6 slices of chopped salami with the tomato and mozzarella to the top of the pizza. Continue as above.

vegetable spaghetti bolognese

Preparation time **15 minutes**
Cooking time **40–45 minutes**
Serves **2**

1 tablespoon **vegetable oil**
1 **onion**, finely chopped
1 **garlic clove**, finely chopped
1 **celery stick**, finely chopped
1 **carrot**, finely chopped
½ cup **chestnut mushrooms**,
  roughly chopped
1 tablespoon **tomato paste**
13 oz can **chopped tomatoes**
1 cup **red wine** or **gluten-free
  vegetable stock**
pinch of **dried mixed herbs**
1 teaspoon **yeast extract**
5 oz **textured vegetable
  protein (TVP)**
2 tablespoons chopped
  parsley
7 oz **gluten-free spaghetti**
salt and **black pepper**
Parmesan shavings,
  to serve

Heat the oil in a large heavy saucepan over a medium heat. Add the onion, garlic, celery, carrot, and mushrooms and cook, stirring frequently, for 5 minutes or until softened. Add the tomato paste and cook, stirring, for a minute more.

Add the tomatoes, wine or stock, herbs, yeast extract, and TVP. Bring to a boil, then reduce the heat, cover, and simmer for 30–40 minutes until the TVP is tender. Stir in the parsley and season well with salt and pepper.

Cook the pasta in a large saucepan of salted boiling water according to the package instructions until it is al dente. Drain well.

Divide the pasta between 2 serving plates, top with the vegetable mixture, and serve immediately with a sprinkling of grated Parmesan.

For lentil bolognese, make the sauce as above, replacing the mushrooms with 1 cored, deseeded and diced red pepper and ²/₃ cup canned green lentils. Rinse the lentils well before use. If you are using dried lentils, cook them in boiling water first, according to the package instructions, then drain. Cook the spaghetti as above and serve with the sauce, sprinkled with grated Parmesan cheese.

savory
bakes

cheesy herby muffins

Preparation time **5 minutes**
Cooking time **20 minutes**
Makes **8**

6 oz **Gruyère cheese**
3 **scallions**, finely sliced
1 teaspoon **thyme leaves**
1 tablespoon chopped **parsley**
²/₃ cup **rice flour**
½ teaspoon **gluten-free baking powder**
3 cups **fresh gluten-free bread crumbs**
1 teaspoon **gluten-free English mustard**
3 **eggs**, beaten
¼ cup **butter**, melted
4 tablespoons **milk**

Line an 8-cup muffin pan with paper bake cups.

Mix together all the ingredients in a large bowl until just combined and spoon the mixture into the paper cups.

Place in a preheated oven, 170°F, for 20 minutes or until golden and just firm to the touch. Remove from the oven and serve warm.

For caramelized onion & feta muffins, heat 1 tablespoon olive oil in a saucepan, add 1 thinly sliced onion, and fry over a low heat for about 10 minutes until very soft and beginning to brown. Add 1 teaspoon superfine sugar and conpanue to cook for 2–3 minutes. Line a muffin pan as above. Mix together 4 oz crumbled feta cheese, 1 tablespoon chopped thyme and the caramelized onion with the rice flour, baking powder, bread crumbs, mustard, eggs, melted butter, and milk as above. Spoon into the paper cups and place in a preheated oven, 400°F, for 20 minutes until golden and firm to the touch. Serve warm.

chili corn bread

Preparation time **5 minutes**
Cooking time **30–35 minutes**
Makes **16 squares**

1 cup **rice flour**
1 cup **cornmeal**
1 teaspoon **salt**
2 teaspoons **gluten-free baking powder**
1 tablespoon **superfine sugar**
3 tablespoons grated **Parmesan cheese**
handful of **fresh herbs**, chopped
1 **red chili**, seeded, and finely chopped
3 tablespoons **olive oil**, plus extra for oiling
2 **eggs**, beaten
1¼ cups **buttermilk**

Oil an 8 inch square cake pan.

Sift together the flour, polenta, salt, and baking powder into a large bowl. Stir in the sugar, Parmesan, herbs, and chili.

Mix together the oil, eggs, and buttermilk in a separate bowl, then gently stir into the dry ingredients, until combined.

Pour the mixture into the prepared pan and place in a preheated oven, 375°F, for 30–35 minutes until golden. Remove from the oven and transfer to a wire rack to cool, then cut into 16 squares. Delicious served with the Fish Chowder on page 48. The bread is best eaten on the same day.

For bacon & sweetcorn bread, stir a 7 oz can drained corn kernels and 6 broiled chopped bacon slices into the dry ingredients and continue as above.

feta & herb loaf

Preparation time **10 minutes**, plus rising
Cooking time **45 minutes**
Makes **1 x 2 lb loaf**

vegetable oil, for oiling
1¼ cups **cornmeal**
⅔ cup **rice flour**
½ cup **dried milk powder**
pinch of **salt**
¼ oz envelope **quick-rising active dry yeast**
2 teaspoons **superfine sugar**
2 teaspoons **xanthan gum**
3 **eggs**, beaten
2 tablespoons chopped **fresh herbs**
1¾ cups **hand-hot water**
4 oz **feta cheese**, crumbled

Oil and line a 2 lb loaf pan.

Sift together the cornmeal, flour, milk powder, and salt in a large bowl and stir well to combine. Stir in the yeast, sugar, and xanthan gum.

Mix together the eggs, herbs, and water in a separate bowl, add to the dry ingredients, and combine to form a smooth mixture. Beat for 5 minutes, then stir in the feta.

Spoon the mixture into the prepared pan, cover with a clean damp dish towel, and leave in a warm place to rise for about 30 minutes, until the mixture is near the top of the pan.

Place in a preheated oven, 350°F, for about 45 minutes or until the loaf is brown and sounds hollow when tapped on the bottom. Remove from the oven and transfer to a wire rack to cool.

For pesto & parmesan bread, make as above, replacing the feta with 2 tablespoons grated Parmesan cheese. Stir 2 tablespoons pesto into the egg and water mixture before adding to the dry ingredients. Continue as above.

nutty seed loaf

Preparation time **10 minutes**
Cooking time **25 minutes**
Makes **8 pieces**

2½ cups **brown rice flour**,
   plus extra for dusting
¼ cup **rice bran**
2 tablespoons **nonfat dried
   milk powder**
½ teaspoon **baking soda**
1 teaspoon **gluten-free
   baking powder**
½–1 teaspoon **salt**
1 teaspoon **xanthan gum**
pinch of **superfine sugar**
½ cup mixed **sunflower** and
   pumpkin seeds
½ cup **hazelnuts**, toasted and
   roughly chopped
1 **egg**, lightly beaten
1¼ cups **buttermilk**

Stir together all the dry ingredients, including the nuts, in a large bowl. Mix together the egg and buttermilk in a separate bowl, add to the dry ingredients, and combine to form a soft dough.

Turn the dough out onto a surface lightly dusted with rice flour and form into a round about 8 inches in diameter. Mark into 8 segments, then place on a baking sheet and dust with a little extra rice flour.

Place in an oven preheated to its highest setting and bake for 10 minutes, then reduce the heat to 400°F, and continue to cook for about 15 minutes until the loaf is golden and sounds hollow when tapped on the bottom. Remove from the oven and transfer to a wire rack to cool.

For fruity seed loaf, make the dough as above, adding ⅔ cup chopped dried figs and 6 chopped ready-to-eat dried apricots to the dry ingredients. Form into a round and bake as above, then brush the top of the loaf with 1 tablespoon of honey.

parmesan, olive, & tomato loaf

Preparation time 10 minutes,
plus rising
Cooking time **45 minutes**
Makes **1 x 2 lb loaf**

vegetable oil, for oiling
1 ¼ cups **cornmeal**
⅔ cup **rice flour**
½ cup **dried milk powder**
pinch of **salt**
¼ oz envelope **quick-rising
active dry yeast**
2 teaspoons **superfine sugar**
2 teaspoons **xanthan gum**
3 **eggs**, beaten
2 tablespoons **sundried
tomato paste**
1 ¾ cups **hand-hot water**
½ cup grated **Parmesan
cheese**
⅓ cup pitted **olives**, chopped
2 teaspoons chopped
oregano

Oil and line a 2 lb loaf pan.

Sift together the cornmeal, flour, milk powder, and salt into a large bowl and stir well to combine. Stir in the yeast, sugar, and xanthan gum.

Mix together the eggs, tomato paste, and water in a separate bowl, add to the dry ingredients, and combine to form a smooth mixture. Beat for 5 minutes, then stir in the remaining ingredients.

Spoon the mixture into the prepared pan, cover with a clean damp dish towel, and leave in a warm place to rise for about 30 minutes until the mixture is near the top of the pan.

Place in a preheated oven, 350°F, for about 45 minutes or until it is brown and sounds hollow when tapped on the bottom. Remove from the oven and transfer to a wire rack to cool.

For apple & walnut bread, make the dough as above, omitting the sundried tomato paste and replacing the Parmesan, olives, and oregano with 1 large peeled and grated dessert apple and ¾ cup chopped walnuts. Leave to prove and then bake as above.

potato & thyme griddle scones

Preparation time **10 minutes**
Cooking time **15 minutes**
Makes **6**

8 oz **potato**, peeled and cut
  into ¾ inch cubes
2 tablespoons **butter**, plus
  extra for cooking
⅓ cup **rice flour**, plus extra
  for dusting
1 teaspoon **gluten-free
  baking powder**
1 teaspoon **thyme**, chopped,
  plus extra sprigs to garnish
  (optional)
2 tablespoons **buttermilk**
1 **egg**, beaten
vegetable oil, for brushing
salt

Cook the potatoes in a saucepan of salted boiling water for 10 minutes or until tender. Drain well.

Place the potato and butter in a large bowl and mash together until smooth, then stir in the remaining ingredients together with a pinch of salt, until combined. Bring the mixture together to form a ball.

Turn the dough out onto a surface lightly dusted with rice flour, roll into a round about ¼ inch thick, and cut into 6 triangles.

Brush a griddle or nonstick skillet with a little oil and add a knob of butter, then cook the scones for 2–3 minutes on each side until golden. Serve warm, garnished with thyme sprigs if liked, and with butter and cheese.

For cheesy potato, garlic & chive cakes, stir 3 oz crumbled Cheshire cheese into the potato mixture together with 1 crushed garlic clove and 1 teaspoon chopped chives in place of the thyme. Form into 6 rounds about ¼ inch thick and cook as above.

garlic & caramelized onion bhajis

Preparation **10 minutes**,
  plus standing
Cooking time **15 minutes**
Serves **6**

2 tablespoons **olive oil**
1 **onion**, sliced
2 **garlic cloves**, sliced
1 teaspoon **cumin seeds**
2 tablespoons chopped
  cilantro
1¼ cups **chickpea flour**
1 teaspoon **baking soda**
½ teaspoon **salt**
1 cup **water**

Heat half the oil in a nonstick skillet, add the onion, garlic, and cumin and fry for 5–6 minutes until the onion is golden and softened. Stir in the cilantro.

Meanwhile, mix together the flour, baking soda, salt, and water in a bowl and set aside for 10 minutes, then stir in the onion mixture.

Heat a little of the remaining oil in the skillet, add spoonfuls of the onion mixture, fry for 2–3 minutes, and turn halfway through cooking. Transfer to a serving plate and keep warm while frying the remainder of the mixture.

For spicy spinach & onion bhajis, make as above, adding ¼ cup cooked and well-squeezed chopped spinach to the skillet with the cilantro. Add ½ teaspoon dried red pepper flakes flakes to the flour mixture, then continue as above.

corn & bacon muffins

Preparation time **10 minutes**
Cooking time **20–25 minutes**
Makes **12**

6 **bacon slices**, finely chopped
1 small **red onion**, finely
   chopped
1 cup **frozen corn kernels**
1 cup **fine cornmeal**
1 cup **gluten-free all-purpose
   flour**
2 teaspoons **gluten-free
   baking powder**
½ cup grated
cheddar cheese
¾ cup **milk**
2 **eggs**
3 tablespoons **vegetable oil**,
   plus extra for greasing

Oil a 12-cup muffin tray.

Heat a skillet, add the bacon and onion and dry-fry
for 3–4 minutes until the bacon is turning crisp.

Cook the corn in a saucepan of boiling water for
2 minutes to soften. Drain well.

Mix together the cornmeal, flour, and baking powder in
a bowl, then stir in the corn, cheese, bacon, and onion.
Mix together the milk, eggs, and oil in a separate bowl,
add to the dry ingredients, and stir gently to combine.

Pour the mixture into the oiled holes and place in a
preheated oven, 425°F, for 15–20 minutes until golden
and just firm to the touch. Remove from the oven and
transfer to a wire rack to cool.

For cheese & corn muffins, omit the bacon and
fry the onion in 1 tablespoon olive oil. Continue as
above, adding an extra ¼ cup cheddar cheese to the
dry ingredients and 1 teaspoon smoked paprika, and
season well. Bake as above.

pizza scrolls

Preparation time **25 minutes,
plus rising**
Cooking time **12–15 minutes**
Makes **8**

2 x ¼ oz envelopes **quick-
rising active dry yeast**
1 teaspoon **superfine sugar**
1 cup **milk**, warmed
1 cup **rice flour**, plus extra for
dusting
⅔ cup **potato flour**
1 teaspoon **gluten-free
baking powder**
1 teaspoon **xanthan gum**
pinch of **salt**
1 tablespoon **sunflower oil**,
plus extra for oiling
1 **egg**, beaten

Filling
4 tablespoons **puréed
tomatoes**
2 cups mixed grated
mozzarella and **cheddar
cheese**
3 oz **wafer-thin ham**,
shredded
handful of **basil**, chopped

Put the yeast, sugar, and milk in a bowl and set aside
for about 10 minutes until frothy. Stir together the flours,
baking powder, xanthan gum, and salt in a large bowl.

Mix together the oil and egg in a separate bowl, stir into
the yeast mixture and add this to the dry ingredients.
Combine to form a soft dough.

Turn the dough out onto a surface lightly dusted with
rice flour and knead for 5 minutes, adding a little rice
flour if the mixture becomes sticky. Place in a lightly
oiled bowl, cover with a clean damp dish towel, and
leave in a warm place to rise for about 40 minutes or
until well risen.

Roll the dough out on the floured surface to a rectangle
approximately 12 x 10 inches, spread with the puréed
tomatoes, then sprinkle over the remaining filling
ingredients. Roll the pizza up from one long edge,
then slice into 8 pieces.

Place the rolled-up pizza scrolls side by side on a lightly
oiled heavy baking sheet or pan. They should be pushed
up against each other so that the sides are touching.
Place in a preheated oven, 425°F, for 12–15 minutes
until golden. Remove from the oven and serve warm.

For olive & artichoke pizza scrolls, make and roll
out the dough as above. For the filling, spread over
2 tablespoons olive tapenade or sundried tomato
paste. Sprinkle with 6 drained and thinly sliced bottled
artichoke hearts, 5 oz roughly chopped mozzarella
cheese, and 6 drained and sliced sundried tomatoes
in oil. Roll up and bake as above.

spicy fruit & seed bread

Preparation time **10 minutes**, plus rising
Cooking time **20–25 minutes**
Makes **1 x 1 lb loaf**

1 cup **gram flour**
1¼ cups **gluten-free flour**
2 teaspoons **quick-rising active dry yeast**
1 teaspoon **salt**
1 teaspoon **superfine sugar**
1 tablespoon **black onion seeds**
1 tablespoon **cumin seeds**
2 teaspoons **ground cilantro**
¼ teaspoon **dried red pepper flakes**
2 oz **dried mango** or **pear**, chopped
2 tablespoons **peanut oil**, plus extra for oiling
¾ cup **hand-hot water**

Grease a 1 lb loaf pan.

Place the flours, yeast, salt, sugar, spices, and dried fruit in a bowl and stir to combine. Mix together the oil and water in a separate bowl, add to the dry ingredients, and combine to form a stiff dough.

Spoon the mixture into the prepared pan, cover with a clean damp dish towel, and leave in a warm place to rise for about 45 minutes or until the mixture is slightly above the top of the pan.

Place in a preheated oven, 400°F, for 20–25 minutes until firm to the touch. Remove from the oven and transfer to a wire rack to cool. Serve cut into slices spread with butter, if liked.

For toasted fruity bread with blackberries & plums,
heat 2 tablespoons butter in a nonstick saucepan, add 4 halved and stoned plums, and fry over a gentle heat until slightly softened. Stir in 1 up blackberries and 1 tablespoon superfine sugar and cook for an additional 1–2 minutes until the sugar has dissolved and the blackberries are beginning to release their juices. Meanwhile, toast 4 slices of Spicy Fruit & Seed Bread (see above) and butter lightly. Serve the fruit on the toast.

desserts

hazelnut meringue stack

Preparation time **10 minutes,** plus cooling

Cooking time **45 minutes**

Serves **8**

4 **egg whites**

8 oz **superfine sugar**

1 teaspoon **white wine vinegar**

1 1/3 cups **blanched hazelnuts,** toasted and roughly chopped

3/4 cup **heavy cream**

2 1/4 cups **raspberries**

cocoa powder, for dusting

Line 3 baking sheets with nonstick parchment paper.

Whisk the egg whites in a large clean bowl until they form stiff peaks. Add the sugar a spoonful at a time and continue to whisk until thick and glossy. Fold in the vinegar with a large metal spoon.

Fold half the hazelnuts into the mixture, then divide it between the prepared sheets, spooning the meringue into 3 rounds roughly 7 inches in diameter.

Place in a preheated oven, 300°F for 45 minutes, then switch off the oven and allow the meringue to cool.

Whip the cream in a bowl until it forms soft peaks, spoon the cream over 2 of the meringues and top each with the raspberries and remaining nuts, reserving a few raspberries for decoration.

Stack the meringues with the plain one on top, then dust with a little cocoa powder and decorate with the remaining raspberries. Serve on the same day or chill for up to 2 days.

For banana, chocolate & fudge meringue, make the meringues as above. Fold 2 chopped bananas into the whipped cream with 3 1/2 oz grated gluten-free plain dark chocolate and 3 1/2 oz chopped fudge pieces. Sandwich the meringues together with the whipped cream mixture as above, and decorate with gluten-free plain dark chocolate shavings or curls.

pear, apple, & cinnamon crumble

Preparation time **10 minutes**
Cooking time **30–35 minutes**
Serves **4**

1 1/2 lb **pears**, peeled, cored,
   and sliced
1 lb **cooking apples**, peeled,
   cored, and sliced
2 tablespoons **light brown
   sugar**
1 teaspoon **ground cinnamon**
4 tablespoons **apple juice**

Topping
1 1/3 cups **rice flour**
1/2 cup **butter**, cubed
1/2 cup **light brown sugar**
1/4 cup **slivered almonds**
3 tablespoons **blanched
   hazelnuts**, roughly chopped

Put the pears and apples in a large saucepan with the sugar, cinnamon, and apple juice. Cover and cook gently, stirring occasionally, for about 10 minutes or until the fruit is just tender. Transfer to an ovenproof dish.

Make the topping. Place the flour and butter in a food processor and whiz until the mixture resembles fine bread crumbs. Alternatively, place the flour in a large bowl, add the butter and rub in with the fingertips until the mixture resembles fine bread crumbs. Stir in the sugar and nuts, then sprinkle over the fruit and press down gently.

Place in a preheated oven 400°F for 20–25 minutes until golden and bubbling. Serve with sour cream or cream.

For rhubarb & ginger crumble, cut 2 lb rhubarb into chunks and put in an ovenproof dish with 2 tablespoons water and 6 tablespoons superfine sugar. Place in a preheated oven 400°F for 15 minutes, then stir in 1 teaspoon ground ginger. Make the topping as above, adding 4 oz finely chopped marzipan. Sprinkle over the rhubarb and bake in the oven as above.

lemony cheesecake

Preparation time **10 minutes**, plus chilling

Serves **6**

1½ cups crushed **gluten-free plain** or **ginger cookies**
¼ cup **butter**, melted
1 cup **mascarpone cheese**
grated zest and juice of 2 **lemons**
⅔ cup **heavy cream**
1 cup **confectioner's sugar**, sifted

To decorate
blueberries and **raspberries**
lemon zest curls

Mix together the crushed cookies and melted butter in a bowl, then press into the base and up the side of an 8 inch fluted loose-bottomed tart pan. Chill in the refrigerator until firm.

Beat together the mascarpone, lemon juice and zest, heavy cream and confectioners' sugar in a large bowl until thick, then spoon over the cookie base. Chill for at least 30 minutes until firm.

Decorate with blueberries, raspberries, and lemon zest curls, when ready to serve.

For lemon & raspberry swirl cheesecake, make the cookie base and mascarpone mixture as above. Whiz together 1½ cups raspberries and 1 tablespoon confectioners' sugar in a food processor or blender and gently fold into the mascarpone mixture. Spoon onto the cookie base and chill until firm. Decorate with a few extra raspberries and serve.

chocolate profiteroles

Preparation time **10 minutes**
Cooking time **30 minutes**
Makes **about 20**

²/₃ cup **water**
¼ cup **butter**, plus extra
   for greasing
¹/₃ cup **rice flour**
1 teaspoon **gluten-free
   baking powder**
½ teaspoon **baking soda**
1 teaspoon **superfine sugar**
2 **eggs**, beaten

Chocolate sauce
7 oz **gluten-free bittersweet
   chocolate**, broken
   into pieces
6 tablespoons **heavy cream**

Cream filling
¾ cup **heavy cream**
1 tablespoon **confectioners'
   sugar**

Put the water and butter in a saucepan and bring to a boil. Sift together the flour, baking powder, sugar, and baking soda into a bowl, then quickly tip into the pan and beat with a hand-held electric mixer. Gradually beat in the eggs until glossy, then spoon the mixture into a pastry bag fitted with a ½ inch plain tip and pipe small mounds on to 2 lightly greased and dampened baking sheets.

Place in a preheated oven, 400°F, for 10 minutes, then increase the temperature to 425°F, and cook for an additional 12–15 minutes until crisp and golden. Remove from the oven, pierce a hole in the side of each of the profiteroles, and transfer to a wire rack to cool.

Make the chocolate sauce. Place the chocolate and cream in a heatproof bowl over a saucepan of simmering water and leave until melted. Stir together and leave to cool a little.

Whip the cream with the confectioners' sugar in a bowl until it forms soft peaks and use to fill each bun. Pile the buns onto a serving dish, then pour over the chocolate sauce.

For coffee profiteroles, make and bake the profiteroles as above. Mix 2 teaspoons instant coffee with 2 teaspoons boiling water. Leave to cool. Stir in 3½ oz mascarpone with 3½ oz whipped cream and 1 tablespoon confectioners' sugar. Use to fill the cooled profiteroles.

easy banoffee pies

Preparation time **5 minutes**
Serves **4**

6 **gluten-free chocolate
cookies**, roughly crushed
13 oz can **gluten-free
caramel sauce**
2 **bananas**, sliced
²/₃ cup **extra-thick heavy
cream**
2 oz **gluten-free bittersweet
chocolate**, shaved or grated

Divide the crushed cookies between 4 tall glasses.

Spoon the caramel into each glass, then cover with the
banana slices.

Top with the cream and decorate with the chocolate.
Serve immediately.

For fudge sundaes, place 2 scoops of gluten-free
vanilla ice cream in each of 4 tall glasses. Mix together
4 oz melted gluten-free milk chocolate and half a
13 oz can caramel sauce in a bowl. Spoon the fudge
over the ice cream, then sprinkle with a handful
of chopped toasted hazelnuts and 1 sliced banana.
Serve immediately.

berry meringue mess

Preparation time **10 minutes**, plus cooling
Cooking time **1 hour**
Serves **6**

4 **egg whites**
1 cup **superfine sugar**
1 teaspoon **white wine vinegar**
1¼ cups **heavy cream**
1½ cups **raspberries**, plus extra, left whole, to decorate
1¼ cups **strawberries**, hulled and quartered, plus extra, left whole and unhulled, to decorate
2 tablespoons **confectioners' sugar**
2 tablespoons **cream liqueur**

Line 2 large baking sheets with nonstick parchment paper.

Whisk the egg whites in a large clean bowl until they form stiff peaks. Add the sugar a spoonful at a time and continue to whisk until thick and glossy. Fold in the vinegar with a large metal spoon.

Spoon or pipe 12 meringues onto the prepared baking sheets. Place in a preheated oven, 300°F, for 1 hour, then switch off the oven and allow the meringues to cool completely. When cool, roughly crush the meringues.

Whip the cream in a large bowl until it forms soft peaks. Roughly crush together the raspberries and strawberries and stir into the cream. Fold in the crushed meringues, confectioners' sugar, and cream liqueur. Spoon into 6 tall glasses, decorate with exta whole berries and serve immediately.

For mango & passion fruit mess, make the meringues as above and roughly crush. Whip the cream with 2 tablespoons confectioners' sugar in a large bowl until it forms soft peaks. Peel and pit 1 large mango and purée half the flesh in a food processor or blender. Chop the remaining mango flesh and stir all the mango into the cream mixture with the scooped flesh of 2 passion fruit. Fold in the crushed meringues and serve immediately.

sticky toffee pudding

Preparation time **10 minutes**, plus soaking

Cooking time **25–30 minutes**

Serves **8**

1 ½ cups pitted and chopped **dried dates**

¾ cup **boiling water**

1 teaspoon **baking soda**

¼ cup **butter**, softened, plus extra for greasing

¼ cup **light brown sugar**

2 **eggs**, beaten

⅔ cup **rice flour**

1 teaspoon **gluten-free baking powder**

To serve

handful of chopped **pecan nuts**

heavy cream

Toffee sauce

1 cup **butter**

1 ¼ cups **soft light brown sugar**

¾ cup **heavy cream**

Put the dates in a heatproof bowl, pour over the boiling water, and stir in the baking soda. Leave to soak for 10 minutes.

Grease and line an 8 inch square cake pan.

Beat together the butter, sugar, eggs, flour, baking powder, and soaked dates and their frothy liquid in a bowl. Pour into the prepared pan. Place in a preheated oven, 350°F, for 25–30 minutes until firm to the touch.

Meanwhile, place all the sauce ingredients in a saucepan and heat through until the sugar has dissolved. Cut the cake into 8 pieces and serve in bowls topped with the sauce, cream, and a sprinkling of pecan nuts.

For sticky ginger loaf cake, make the cake mixture as above, adding 1 ½ teaspoons ground ginger. Pour into a 2 lb greased and lined loaf pan and bake in the oven as above. Heat 1 oz butter, 4 tablespoons light brown sugar, and 2 tablespoons heavy cream in a small saucepan until the sugar has dissolved, then boil for 3 minutes. Leave the cake to cool slightly, then remove from the pan, peel away the lining paper and set on a serving plate. Pour over the sauce, sprinkle with a handful of chopped walnuts, and serve.

baked pears with marzipan

Preparation time **10 minutes**
Cooking time **25–30 minutes**
Serves **4**

4 **pears**, peeled, keeping the
   pears whole
juice of ½ **lemon**
2 oz **marzipan**, grated or
   finely chopped
1 tablespoon **golden raisins**
4 tablespoons **apple juice**
2 tablespoons **honey**
2 tablespoons **slivered
   almonds**, toasted

Core the pears from the bases, leaving the stalks in place, and coat with the lemon juice. Mix together the marzipan and golden raisins in a bowl, then spoon the mixture into the cored cavity of the pears. Stand the stuffed pears in a small ovenproof dish.

Spoon over the apple juice, then drizzle over the honey and place in a preheated oven, 350°F, for 25–30 minutes until tender.

Remove from the oven and sprinkle with the almonds. Serve with whipped cream or custard.

For amaretti-stuffed pears, prepare the pears as above. Mix together 4 chopped apricots, 4 crushed amaretti cookies, the juice of ½ orange, and 1 tablespoon honey or maple syrup. Blend in a food processor or blender and spoon into the pear cavities. Stand the stuffed pears in a small ovenproof dish and bake in the oven as above until tender.

perfect pecan pies

Preparation time **15 minutes, plus chilling**
Cooking time **20–25 minutes**
Makes **8**

½ cup **brown rice flour**, plus extra for dusting
⅓ cup **gram flour**
½ cup **cornmeal**
1 teaspoon **xanthan gum**
½ cup **butter**, cubed
2 tablespoons **superfine sugar**
1 **egg**, beaten

Filling
½ cup **light brown sugar**
⅔ cup **butter**
5 tablespoons **honey**
1½ cups **pecan nut halves**, half roughly chopped
2 **eggs**, beaten

Grease and line 8 individual 4½ inch pie pans with parchment paper. Place the flours, cornmeal, xanthan gum, and butter in a food processor and whiz until the mixture resembles fine bread crumbs. Alternatively, mix together the flours, polenta, and xanthan gum in a large bowl. Add the butter and blend with the fingertips until the mixture resembles fine bread crumbs. Stir in the sugar.

Add the egg and enough cold water to form a dough. Knead for a couple of minutes, then wrap in plastic wrap and chill for about 1 hour.

Meanwhile, place the sugar, butter, and honey for the filling in a saucepan and heat until the sugar has dissolved. Allow to cool for 10 minutes.

Turn the dough out on a surface lightly dusted with rice flour and knead to soften it a little. Divide the dough into 8, then roll each piece out to a thickness of ⅛ inch and use to line the pie pans. Stir the chopped pecans and eggs into the filling mixture and pour into the pastry-lined pans. Arrange the pecan halves over the top.

Place in a preheated oven, 400°F, Gas Mark 6, for 15–20 minutes until the filling is firm. Remove from the oven and allow to cool in the pans.

For homemade vanilla ice cream, to serve as an accompaniment, whip 1¼ cups heavy cream with 2 tablespoons superfine sugar in a bowl until it forms soft peaks. Fold in a 13 oz can ready-made gluten-free custard and 1 teaspoon vanilla extract. Pour into a freezerproof container and freeze for 2 hours, then stir with a fork. Put back in the freezer for at least 6 hours, or until solid, then serve with the pecan pies.

chocolate & chestnut roulade

Preparation time **15 minutes**
Cooking time **20 minutes**
Serves **8**

butter, for greasing
6 **eggs**, separated
½ cup **superfine sugar**
2 tablespoons **unsweetened
    cocoa powder**
confectioners' sugar, for
    dusting

Filling
⅔ cup **heavy cream**
½ cup **chestnut purée** or
    **sweetened chestnut
    spread**

Grease and line an 11½ x 7 inch jelly roll pan.

Whisk the egg whites in a large clean bowl until they form soft peaks. Whisk together the egg yolks and sugar in a separate bowl until thick and pale. Fold the cocoa powder and egg whites into the egg yolk mixture.

Spoon the batter into the prepared pan and place in a preheated oven, 350°F, for 20 minutes. Remove from the oven and cool in the pan.

Turn the cooled cake out onto a piece of waxed paper dusted with confectioners' sugar. Whip the cream for the filling in a large clean bowl until it forms soft peaks. Fold the chestnut purée or sweetened chestnut spread into the cream, then smooth the filling over the cake.

Using the waxed paper to help you, carefully roll up the roulade from one short end and lift it gently onto its serving dish. (Don't worry if it cracks: it won't detract from its appearance or taste.) Dust with confectioners' sugar. Chill until needed and eat on the day it is made.

For chocolate & black cherry roulade, make the cake as above. To make the filling, omit the chestnut purée or spread and replace with a 13 oz can drained black cherries. Spread over the sponge, roll up, and dust with confectioners' sugar as above.

christmas pudding

Preparation time **20 minutes**,
  plus overnight soaking
Cooking time **6 hours**
Serves **6–8**

1 cup **gluten-free suet**
2 tablespoons **rice flour**
4 cups **gluten-free fresh
  bread crumbs**
1 cup **dark brown sugar**
3½ cups mixed **golden
  raisins, raisins,** and
  currants
²/₃ cup **ready-to-eat dried
  apricots**, chopped
2 teaspoons **pumpkin
  pie spice**
1 **apple**, grated
2 large **eggs**
4 tablespoons **brandy**
4 tablespoons **apple juice**
grated zest of **1 orange**
heavy cream, to serve

Mix together all the ingredients in a large bowl, cover, and allow to soak for 24 hours.

Spoon the mixture into a 5 cup pudding mold, cover with a piece of nonstick parchment paper that has been folded with a pleat and secure with string, then cover with foil.

Steam the pudding for about 6 hours, keeping the water topped up in the saucepan so that it does not dry out. When cooked, rewrap the pudding in nonstick parchment paper and foil. Store in a cool place until Christmas time.

When ready to serve, steam the pudding for a further 2 hours as above. Serve hot with heavy cream.

For Christmas pudding ice cream, whisk 1¼ cups heavy cream in a bowl until it forms soft peaks. Stir in a 13 oz can ready-made gluten-free custard, 7 oz crumbled Christmas pudding (see above), and 2 tablespoons brandy. Pour into a freezerproof container and freeze for 2 hours, then stir with a fork. Put back in the freezer for at least 6 hours, or until solid, then serve.

traditional cakes & bakes

strawberry scones

Preparation time **10 minutes**
Cooking time **12 minutes**
Makes **8**

1 cup **rice flour**, plus extra
  for dusting
1/2 cup **potato flour**
1 teaspoon **xanthan gum**
1 teaspoon **gluten-free
  baking powder**
1 teaspoon **baking soda**
1/3 cup **butter**, cubed
3 tablespoons **superfine
  sugar**
1 large **egg**, beaten
3 tablespoons **buttermilk**,
  plus extra for brushing

Filling
1/4 pint **heavy cream**
1 1/4 cups **strawberries**, hulled
  and lightly crushed

Place the flours, xanthan gum, baking powder, baking
soda, and butter in a food processor and whiz until the
mixture resembles fine bread crumbs. Alternatively, mix
together the flours, xanthan gum, baking powder, and
baking soda in a large bowl. Add the butter and blend
with the fingertips until the mixture resembles fine
bread crumbs. Stir in the sugar.

Mix together the egg and buttermilk in a separate bowl,
add to the dry ingredients, and mix to a soft dough.

Turn the dough out on a surface lightly dusted with
rice flour, gently press out to a thickness of 1 inch and
use a 2 inch cutter to stamp out 8 scones, rerolling the
trimmings as necessary.

Put on a baking sheet lightly dusted with rice flour,
brush with a little buttermilk, and place in a preheated
oven, 425°F, for about 12 minutes until risen and
golden. Remove from the oven and transfer to a wire
rack to cool.

Meanwhile, whip the cream in a bowl until it forms
fairly firm peaks and fold in the strawberries. Split the
scones in half and fill with the strawberry cream.

For fruit scones, add 2/3 cup golden raisins and
1/2 teaspoon ground cinnamon to the ingredients in
the food processor before processing or to the dry
ingredients before rubbing in the butter. Continue as
above. Serve the scones warm with butter and jelly,
if desired.

boozy christmas cake

Preparation time **20 minutes, plus soaking**
Cooking time **4–4½ hours**
Serves **12–14**

5¼ cups mixed **golden raisins** and **currants**
½ cup **ready-to-eat dried apricots**, diced
½ cup **candied cherries**, rinsed and halved
grated zest of 2 **oranges**
⅔ cup **brandy**, plus extra to feed and decorate
1 cup **butter**, softened
1 cup **dark brown sugar**
1 tablespoon **molasses**
1½ cups **rice flour**
1 teaspoon **pumpkin pie spice**
4 **eggs**, beaten
⅓ cup **blanched almonds**, cut into slivers

To decorate
3 tablespoons **apricot jelly**
½ cup **pecan nuts**,
2 oz each **blanched almonds, glacé cherries** and **ready-to-eat dried apricots**

Mix together the dried fruit, candied cherries, and orange zest in a bowl and pour over the brandy. Stir well, cover, and allow to soak for 24 hours.

Grease and line an 8 inch round deep cake pan. Wrap and tie a double thickness of brown paper or newspaper around the outside of the pan to come 2 inches above the rim.

Beat the butter and sugar together in a large bowl until light and fluffy. Mix in the molasses. Sift together the flour and spice, then fold into the creamed mixture alternately with a little of the egg until all the flour and eggs are combined. Stir in the soaked fruit, plus any juices, and the almonds.

Spoon the mixture into the prepared pan, ensuring it is pressed right into the base. Cover with a piece of waxed paper with a small hole in the middle. Place in a preheated oven, 275°F, for about 4–4½ hours or until a skewer inserted into the middle of the cake comes out clean. Remove from the oven, remove the paper, and cool in the pan.

Feed the cake by piercing holes in the surface and drizzling with brandy. When cold, remove from the pan, wrap in foil, and store in an airtight container for up to 2 months. Feed about once a week until required.

Place the jelly and 1 tablespoon brandy in a small saucepan over a low heat until melted. Halve the cherries, and apricots, then stir into the pan with the nuts until well coated. Spoon over the cake and allow to set.

coconut & mango cake

Preparation time **10 minutes**
Cooking time **45–50 minutes**
Serves **12**

½ cup **butter**, softened, plus
   extra for greasing
½ cup **light brown sugar**
4 **eggs**, separated
1¾ cups **buttermilk**
1¼ cups **cornmeal**
1⅓ cups **rice flour**
2 teaspoons **gluten-free
   baking powder**
½ cup **coconut milk powder**
⅔ cup **shredded coconut**
1 **mango**, peeled, pitted,
   and puréed

Filling
1 cup **mascarpone cheese**
1 **mango**, peeled, pitted, and
   finely chopped
2 tablespoons **confectioners'
   sugar**

Grease and line a 9 inch round deep cake pan.

Beat together the butter and sugar in a large bowl until light and fluffy, then beat in the egg yolks, buttermilk, cornmeal, flour, baking powder, coconut milk powder, and shredded coconut.

Whisk the egg whites in a large clean bowl until they form soft peaks, then fold into the cake mixture with the puréed mango.

Spoon the batter into the prepared pan and place in a preheated oven, 400°F, for 45–50 minutes until golden and firm to the touch. Remove from the oven and transfer to a wire rack to cool.

When the cake is cool, slice it in half horizontally. Beat together the filling ingredients in a bowl and use half to sandwich the cakes together. Smooth the remaining mixture over the top.

For peach delight cake, make the cake as above, replacing the mango purée with 3 puréed canned peach halves. For the filling, beat together the mascarpone and confectioners's sugar with 2 chopped canned peach halves. Sandwich the cakes together with half the filling mixture and top with the remainder.

chocolate & rum cake

Preparation time **15 minutes**
Cooking time **20–25 minutes**
Serves **16**

5 oz **gluten-free bittersweet
    chocolate**, broken into
    pieces
grated zest and juice of
    1 orange
few drops of **rum essence**
    (optional)
²/₃ cup **unsalted butter**,
    softened, plus extra
    for greasing
²/₃ cup **superfine sugar**
4 **eggs**, separated
1½ cups **ground almonds**

Chocolate frosting
5 oz **gluten-free bittersweet
    chocolate**, broken into
    pieces
½ cup **unsalted butter**

Grease and line 2 x 8 inch layer cake pans.

Place the chocolate, orange zest and juice, and rum
essence, if using, in a heatproof bowl over a saucepan
of simmering water and leave until melted.

Beat together the butter and all but 1 tablespoon of the
sugar in a large bowl until light and fluffy. Beat in the
egg yolks, one by one, then stir in the melted chocolate.

Whisk the egg whites in a large clean bowl until they
form soft peaks. Add the remaining sugar and continue
to whisk until stiff peaks form. Fold the egg whites into
the chocolate mixture with the ground almonds.

Spoon the batter into the prepared pans and place in
a preheated oven, 350°F, for 20–25 minutes, until the
sides are cooked but the center is still a little unset.
Remove from the oven, allow to cool for a few minutes
in the pans, then turn out gently onto a wire rack to
cool completely.

Make the frosting. Melt the chocolate as above, then
whisk in the butter, a tablespoon at a time, until melted.
Remove from the heat and whisk occasionally until cool.
If the frosting is runny, chill until it firms up a little. Fill
and frost the cooled cake with the chocolate mixture.

For crystallized violet petals, whisk 1 egg white and
1 teaspoon water in a bowl until frothy. Place clean
violet petals on a plate, then, using a clean fine paint
brush, gently brush each side of the petals with the
egg white. Dust with superfine sugar and allow to dry
overnight.

victoria layer cake

Preparation time **10 minutes**
Cooking time **20 minutes**
Serves **12**

¾ cup **butter**, softened, plus
   extra for greasing
¾ cup **superfine sugar**
1 cup **brown rice flour**, plus
   extra for dusting
3 **eggs**
1 tablespoon **gluten-free**
   baking powder
few drops of **vanilla extract**
1 tablespoon **milk**

To decorate
4 tablespoons **raspberry jelly**
confectioners' sugar

Grease and flour 2 x 7 inch round cake pans. Place all the cake ingredients in a food processor and whiz until smooth or beat together in a large bowl until light and fluffy.

Spoon the batter into the prepared pans and place in a preheated oven, 400°F, for about 20 minutes until risen and golden. Remove from the oven and transfer to a wire rack to cool.

Sandwich the cooled cakes together with the jelly and dust with confectioners' sugar.

For chocolate cake, make the cakes as above, replacing 1 tablespoon of the rice flour with unsweetened cocoa powder. For the chocolate frosting, dissolve 2 tablespoons unsweetened cocoa powder in 2 tablespoons boiling water and allow to cool. Beat together 3 cups confectioners' sugar and ¾ cup softened butter until light and fluffy, then beat in the cocoa mixture. Use to sandwich together and cover the cooled cakes.

lemon drizzle loaf

Preparation time **10 minutes**
Cooking time **35–40 minutes**
Serves **12**

1 cup **butter**, softened, plus
   extra for greasing
1 cup **superfine sugar**
1½ cups **brown rice flour**
2 teaspoons **gluten-free
   baking powder**
4 **eggs**, beaten
grated zest and juice of
   1 **lemon**

Lemon drizzle
grated zest and juice of
   2 **lemons**
½ cup **granulated sugar**

Grease and line a 2 lb loaf pan.

Place all the cake ingredients in a food processor and whiz until smooth or beat together in a large bowl until light and fluffy.

Spoon the batter into the prepared pan and place in a preheated oven, 350°F, for 35–40 minutes until golden and firm to the touch. Remove from the oven and transfer to a wire rack.

Prick holes all over the cake with a toothpick. Mix together the drizzle ingredients in a bowl, then drizzle the liquid over the warm loaf. Leave until completely cold. To serve, decorate with a twist of lemon peel, if desired.

For orange & apricot loaf, place 1 cup dried ready-to-eat apricots, chopped, and the juice of 1 orange in a saucepan and simmer for 5 minutes, then leave to cool. Meanwhile, make the cake mixture as above, replacing the lemon zest and juice with the grated zest of 1 orange. Stir in the soaked apricots and any juice, spoon into the prepared pan and bake as above. Mix the grated zest and juice of 1 large orange and ½ cup granulated sugar together and drizzle over the top of the warm loaf as above.

tropical fruit cake

Preparation time **15 minutes,
  plus soaking**
Cooking time **1½–2 hours**
Serves **14**

grated zest and juice of
  2 **oranges**
grated zest of 1 **lemon**
2 cups **raisins**
3 cups **dried tropical fruit,**
  chopped
1 tablespoon **candied ginger,**
  chopped
3 tablespoons **brandy**
1 cup **butter,** softened, plus
  extra for greasing
1 cup **light brown sugar**
²⁄₃ cup **soya flour**
¾ cup **rice flour**
1 teaspoon **ground pumpkin
  pie spice**
¾ cup **ground almonds**
4 **eggs,** beaten

To decorate
10 oz **dried fruit** or **nuts**
2 tablespoons **apricot jelly,**
  sieved and warmed

Mix together the orange zest and juice, lemon zest, raisins, dried fruit, and ginger in a bowl and pour over the brandy. Stir well, cover, and allow to soak overnight.

Grease and line an 7 inch square or an 8 inch round deep cake pan Wrap and tie a double thickness of brown paper or newspaper around the outside of the pan to come 2 inches above the rim.

Beat together the butter and sugar in a bowl until light and fluffy. Sift together the flours and spice in a separate bowl and stir in the ground almonds. Gradually add the eggs to the creamed mixture, adding a little flour mixture if it begins to curdle. Fold in the remaining flour mixture and the soaked fruit and any juice.

Spoon the mixture into the prepared pan and place in a preheated oven, 325°F, for 1½–2 hours or until a skewer inserted into the middle of the cake comes out clean. Remove from the oven, remove the paper, and transfer to a wire rack to cool.

Decorate the cooled cake with the dried fruit or nuts and glaze with the apricot jelly.

For traditionally iced fruit cake, make the marzipan by mixing together 3 cups confectioners' sugar, 3 cups ground almonds, 2 lightly beaten egg whites, and 1 teaspoon almond extract in a bowl. Add a little extra confectioners' sugar if it is too sticky. Form into a ball and chill overnight. Make and bake the cake as above. Once cooled, cover with the rolled out marzipan, then top with royal icing and decorate as desired.

beet speckled cake

Preparation time **15 minutes**
Cooking time **45–50 minutes**
Serves **10**

1 cup **butter,** melted, plus
  extra for greasing
1 cup **light brown sugar**
1¼ cups peeled and grated
  raw beets
1 cup toasted and chopped
  whole mixed nuts
3 **eggs**, separated
1 teaspoon **gluten-free
  baking powder**
½ teaspoon **ground
  cinnamon**
grated zest and juice of
  1 **orange**
1¼ cups **rice flour**
3 tablespoons **ground
  almonds**

To decorate
¾ cup **cream cheese**
1 tablespoon **confectioners'
  sugar**
1¼ cups **whole mixed nuts**

Grease an 8 inch round deep cake pan.

Whisk together the melted butter and sugar in a large bowl until pale. Stir in the beets, two-thirds of the nuts, and the egg yolks.

Stir together the baking powder, cinnamon, orange zest and juice, rice flour, and ground almonds in a separate bowl. Add to the beet mixture and beat until smooth.

Whisk the egg whites in a large clean bowl until they form soft peaks, then fold into the beet mixture.

Spoon the mixture into the prepared pan and place in a preheated oven, 400°F, for 45–50 minutes until firm to the touch. Remove from the oven and transfer to a wire rack to cool.

Beat together the cream cheese and confectioners' sugar in a bowl, then smooth the frosting over the top of the cooled cake. Decorate with the whole nuts.

For chocolate beet cake, make the cake mixture as above and fold in 3½ oz chopped gluten-free plain bittersweet chocolate. Bake as above and leave to cool. Top the cake with grated gluten-free plain dark chocolate.

small cakes, cookies, & traybakes

chocolate caramel shortbread

Preparation time **20 minutes**,
plus chilling
Cooking time **15 minutes**
Makes **15**

½ cup **butter**, softened, plus
extra for greasing
¼ cup **superfine sugar**
⅔ cup **brown rice flour**
⅔ cup **cornstarch**

Caramel
½ cup **butter**
¼ cup **light brown sugar**
13 oz **can condensed milk**

Topping
4 oz **gluten-free white
chocolate**
4 oz **gluten-free bittersweet
chocolate**

Grease an 11 x 7 inch baking pan.

Beat together the butter and sugar in a large bowl until light and fluffy, then stir in the flours until well combined.

Press the shortbread into the prepared pan and place in a preheated oven, 400°F, for 10–12 minutes until golden.

Place the caramel ingredients in a heavy saucepan while the shortbread is cooking, and heat over a low heat until the sugar has dissolved, then cook for 5 minutes, stirring continuously. Remove from the heat and allow to cool a little. Remove the shortbread base from the oven, then pour the caramel over and allow to cool and set.

Place the white and dark chocolate in separate heatproof bowls over saucepans of simmering water and leave until melted. When the caramel is firm, spoon alternate spoonfuls of the white and dark chocolate over the caramel, tap the pan on the work surface so that the different chocolates join, then use a knife to make swirls in the chocolate.

Chill until set, then cut the shortbread into 15 squares.

For white chocolate & orange shortbread, make the shortbread base as above, adding the grated zest of 1 orange and ⅔ cup gluten-free white chocolate chips to the mixture. Press into the prepared pan and bake as above. Leave to cool then cut into 15 pieces.

bakewell slice

Preparation time **20 minutes**
Cooking time **20–25 minutes**
Makes **12**

½ cup **cornmeal**
½ cup **brown rice flour**
½ teaspoon **xanthan gum**
½ cup **butter**, cubed, plus
  extra for greasing
grated zest of 1 **lemon**
1 tablespoon **superfine sugar**
1 **egg yolk**, beaten
4 tablespoons **raspberry jelly**
½ cup **slivered almonds**,
  toasted

Cake
2 **eggs**
½ cup **superfine sugar**
¾ cup **rice flour**
½ cup **butter**, softened
½ cup **ground almonds**
1 teaspoon **gluten-free**
  baking powder

Grease an 11 x 7 inch deep baking pan.

Place the cornmeal, flour, xanthan gum, lemon zest, butter, and sugar in a food processor and whiz until the mixture resembles fine bread crumbs. Alternatively, mix together the cornmeal, flour, and xanthan gum in a large bowl. Add the butter and rub in with the fingertips until the mixture resembles fine bread crumbs. Stir in the lemon rind and sugar.

Add the egg yolk and enough cold water to form a dough. Press the pastry into the prepared pan and spread over the jelly.

Place all the cake ingredients in a food processor and whiz until smooth or beat together in a large bowl until light and fluffy.

Spoon the batter into the baking pan and place in a preheated oven, 400°F, for 20–25 minutes until just firm to the touch.

Remove from the oven and allow to cool in the pan. Sprinkle with the toasted almonds and cut into 12 slices.

For chocolate Bakewell tart, make the pastry base as above and use to line the pan. Prick the pastry base with a fork and place in the preheated oven for 10 minutes. Make the cake mixture as above, adding ¼ cup unsweetened cocoa powder, the grated zest of 1 orange, and 2 tablespoons milk. Spoon into the tart shell and bake in the oven as above.

chewy nutty chocolate brownies

Preparation time **10 minutes**
Cooking time **30 minutes**
Makes **15**

$\frac{1}{2}$ cup **butter**, plus extra
   for greasing
3 oz **gluten-free bittersweet
   chocolate**, broken
   into pieces
1 cup **light brown sugar**
2 **eggs**, beaten
few drops of **vanilla extract**
$\frac{1}{2}$ cup **ground almonds**
3 tablespoons **brown rice
   flour**
1$\frac{1}{4}$ cups **mixed nuts**, toasted
   and roughly chopped
vanilla ice cream, to serve

Grease and line an 11 x 7 inch baking pan.

Place the chocolate and butter in a large heatproof
bowl over a saucepan of simmering water and leave
until melted. Stir in all the remaining ingredients and
combine well.

Pour the mixture into the prepared pan and place in
a preheated oven, 350°F, for 30 minutes until slightly
springy in the center.

Remove from the oven and leave to cool for 10
minutes in the pan, then cut into 15 squares. Serve
with a generous dollop of vanilla ice cream.

For macadamia & white chocolate brownies, omit
the bittersweet chocolate and melt the butter in a
saucepan. Stir in 4 oz gluten-free white chocolate, cut
into chunks, with the remaining ingredients, replacing
the mixed nuts with 1 cup roughly chopped macadamia
nuts. Pour into the prepared pan and bake as above.

pistachio & choc chip shortbread

Preparation time **10 minutes**
Cooking time **20 minutes**
Makes **12**

1/2 cup **butter**, softened, plus
extra for greasing
1/4 cup **superfine sugar**
2/3 cup **rice flour**
2/3 cup **cornstarch**
1/4 cup **gluten-free dark
chocolate chips** or chopped
**gluten-free bittersweet
chocolate**
1/2 cup **pistachio nuts**,
chopped
3 oz **gluten-free bittersweet
chocolate**, melted, to
decorate

Grease an 11 x 7 inch baking pan.

Beat together the butter and sugar in a large bowl until light and fluffy. Stir in the flours, chocolate chips or chopped chocolate, and pistachios until well combined.

Press the mixture into the prepared pan and place in a preheated oven, 350°F, for 20 minutes until golden.

Remove from the oven and mark into 12 triangles, then transfer to a wire rack to cool completely before removing from the pan. (It is sometimes easier to remove the shortbread from the pan once it has been chilled a little.)

Drizzle with the melted chocolate. Leave to set, then separate into triangles. Store in an airtight container.

For macadamia & white chocolate brownies, make the mixture as above, replacing the pistachios with 1/3 cup chopped macadamia nuts and 1/4 cup chopped gluten-free white chocolate. Continue as above.

cherry crumble muffins

Preparation time **10 minutes**
Cooking time **20 minutes**
Makes **12**

1½ cups **brown rice flour**
1 teaspoon **baking soda**
2 teaspoons **gluten-free baking powder**
½ cup **superfine sugar**
10 oz can **black cherries**, drained
⅓ cup **butter**, melted
2 **eggs**, beaten
⅔ cup **buttermilk**

Topping
1 tablespoon **ground almonds**
1 tablespoon **light brown sugar**
1 tablespoon **brown rice flour**
1 tablespoon **butter**

Line a large 12-cup muffin pan with large paper bake cups.

Sift together the flour, baking soda, and baking powder in a large bowl, then stir in the sugar.

Mix together the cherries, melted butter, eggs, and buttermilk in a separate bowl, add to the dry ingredients, and stir gently to combine. Spoon the mixture into the paper cups.

Place the topping ingredients in a food processor and whiz until the mixture resembles fine bread crumbs. Alternatively, mix together the ground almonds, sugar, and flour in a bowl. Add the butter and rub in with the fingertips until the mixture resembles fine bread crumbs. Sprinkle over the muffin mixture.

Place in a preheated oven, 350°F, for 20 minutes until golden and firm to the touch. Remove from the oven and transfer to a wire rack to cool.

For banana fudge muffins, make the muffin mixture as above, replacing the cherries with 2 small chopped bananas and 4 oz chopped fudge. Instead of the crumble topping, place 1 banana chip and 1 small piece of fudge on top of each muffin, then bake in the oven as above.

lemon & raspberry cupcakes

Preparation time **10 minutes**
Cooking time **12–15 minutes**
Makes **12**

$^2/_3$ cup **butter**, softened
$^2/_3$ cup **superfine sugar**
$^1/_2$ cup **rice flour**
$^1/_2$ cup **cornstarch**
1 tablespoon **gluten-free baking powder**
grated zest and juice of
　1 **lemon**
3 **eggs**, beaten
1 cup **raspberries**
1 tablespoon **gluten-free lemon curd**

Line a large 12-cup muffin pan with large paper bake cups.

Whisk together all the ingredients except the raspberries and the lemon curd in a large bowl. Fold in the raspberries.

Spoon half of the batter into the paper cups, dot over a little lemon curd, then add the remaining batter.

Place in a preheated oven, 400°F, for 12–15 minutes until golden and firm to the touch. Remove from the oven and transfer to a wire rack to cool.

For citrusy muffins, make as above, adding the grated zest of 1 orange to the mixture. Omit the raspberries and lemon curd and cook as above. Mix 1 ¼ cups confectioners' sugar and 1–2 teaspoons lemon juice in a bowl to make a fairly thick icing and drizzle over the cooled muffins. Decorate with gluten-free lemon and orange gummy candies, if desired.

lavender cupcakes

Preparation time **10 minutes**
Cooking time **13–20 minutes**
Makes **12**

1 tablespoon **milk**
1 teaspoon **lavender flowers**
  (flowerheads only)
1/2 cup **superfine sugar**
1/2 cup **butter**, softened
2/3 cup **rice flour**
1 tablespoon **gram flour**
2 **eggs**, beaten
2 tablespoons **ground almonds**
1 teaspoon **gluten-free baking powder**
1 teaspoon **xanthan gum**

To decorate
1 cup **confectioners' sugar**
12 small **lavender flowerheads**

Line a 12-cup muffin pan with paper bake cups.

Place the milk and lavender in a ramekin, cover with plastic wrap, and microwave on full power for 10 seconds. Remove and leave for 10 minutes to allow the flavors to develop.

Place all the cake ingredients, including the lavender-infused milk, in a food processor and whiz until smooth or beat together in a large bowl.

Spoon the batter into the paper cups and place in a preheated oven, 350°F, for 12–15 minutes until golden and just firm to the touch. Remove from the oven and transfer to a wire rack to cool.

Add a few drops of water to the confectioners' sugar—just enough to make a stiff icing. Smooth a little over each cake and decorate with a lavender flowerhead.

For lavender orange cupcakes, add the grated zest of 1 orange to the milk and lavender and continue to make the cupcakes as above. Bake and cool the cupcakes, as above, then use a little orange juice instead of water to make up the icing. Spread over the cakes and decorate with orange zest curls.

fruity mango bars

Preparation time **10 minutes**
Cooking time **35 minutes**
Makes **12**

½ cup **light brown sugar**

²/₃ cup **butter**, plus extra
for greasing

2 tablespoons **corn syrup**

2 cups **millet flakes**

2 tablespoons mixed **pumpkin**
and **sunflower seeds**

3 oz **dried mango**, roughly
chopped

Grease an 11 x 7 inch baking pan.

Place the sugar, butter, and syrup in a heavy saucepan and heat until melted, then stir in the remaining ingredients.

Spoon the mixture into the prepared pan, press down lightly and place in a preheated oven, 300°F, for 30 minutes.

Remove from the oven and mark into 12 bars, then place on a wire rack to cool completely before removing from the pan and breaking into bars.

For blueberry & hazelnut bars, heat the sugar, butter, and syrup until melted as above. Stir in the millet flakes with ⅓ cup dried blueberries, and ¾ cup chopped toasted hazelnuts. Spoon the mixture into the pan and bake as above.

chocolate chip cookies

Preparation time **10 minutes**
Cooking time **10 minutes**
Makes **30**

$^1/_3$ cup **butter**, softened, plus
    extra for greasing
$^1/_2$ cup **superfine sugar**
$^1/_3$ cup **light brown sugar**
1 **egg**, beaten
1 cup **brown rice flour**, plus
    extra for dusting
$^1/_2$ teaspoon **baking soda**
1 tablespoon **unsweetened**
    cocoa powder
$^1/_2$ cup **gluten-free dark**
    chocolate chips

Grease 3 baking sheets.

Put all the ingredients except the chocolate chips in a food processor and whiz until smooth or beat together in a large bowl. Stir in the chocolate chips, then bring the mixture together to form a ball.

Turn the dough out on a surface lightly dusted with rice flour and divide into 30 balls. Place on the prepared sheets, well spaced apart, pressing down gently with the back of a fork.

Place in a preheated oven, 350°F, for 8–10 minutes. Remove from the oven, leave for a few minutes to harden, then transfer to a wire rack to cool.

For crunchy ginger cookies, make the dough as above, replacing the cocoa powder and chocolate chips with 2 teaspoons ground ginger. Continue as above, sprinkling a little Demerara sugar over the cookies once they have been pressed down with a fork. Cook as above.

orange & cornmeal cookies

Preparation time **10 minutes**, plus chilling
Cooking time **8 minutes**
Makes **20**

½ cup **cornmeal**
3 tablespoons **rice flour**
¼ cup **ground almonds**
½ teaspoon **gluten-free baking powder**
¾ cup **confectioners' sugar**
¼ cup **butter**, cubed
1 **egg yolk**, beaten
grated zest of **1 orange**
¼ cup **slivered almonds**

Line 2 baking sheets with nonstick parchment paper.

Place the cornmeal, flour, ground almonds, baking powder, confectioners' sugar, and butter in a food processor and whiz until the mixture resembles fine bread crumbs or blend by hand in a large bowl. Alternatively, mix together the polenta, flour, ground almonds, baking powder, and icing sugar in a large bowl. Add the butter and rub in with the fingertips until the mixture resembles fine breadcrumbs.

Add the egg yolk and orange zest and combine to form a firm dough. Wrap in plastic wrap and chill for 30 minutes.

Turn the dough out on a surface lightly dusted with rice flour, roll out thinly, and use a 1½ inch cutter to cut out 20 cookies, rerolling the trimmings as necessary. Transfer to the prepared baking sheets and sprinkle with the flaked almonds.

Place in a preheated oven, 350°F, for about 8 minutes until golden. Remove from the oven, leave for a few minutes to harden, then transfer to a wire rack to cool.

For coconut cookies, make the dough as above, adding ⅔ cup toasted shredded coconut. Omit the orange zest and add a little extra egg yolk if the mixture is too dry. Roll into a long sausage shape, wrap in plastic wrap and chill for 30 minutes. Cut thin slices of the dough, place on the prepared baking sheets, and bake as above.

orange animal cookies

Preparation time **10 minutes**
Cooking time **10 minutes**
Makes **20**

1 ¹/₃ cups **brown rice flour**,
  plus extra for dusting
¹/₂ teaspoon **xanthan gum**
1 teaspoon **gluten-free
  baking powder**
¹/₄ cup **light brown sugar**
grated zest of **1 orange**
¹/₄ cup **butter**, cubed
1 **egg**, beaten
2 tablespoons **corn syrup**

To decorate
1 ¹/₄ cups **confectioners'
  sugar**
1 tablespoon **boiling water**
food coloring (optional)
gluten-free candies (optional)

Line 2 baking sheets with nonstick parchment paper.

Place the flour, xanthan gum, baking powder, sugar, orange zest, and butter in a food processor and whizz until the mixture resembles fine bread crumbs or blend by hand in a large bowl. Alternatively, mix together the flour, xanthan gum, and baking powder in a large bowl. Add the butter and rub in with the fingertips until the mixture resembles bread crumbs. Stir in the sugar and orange rind.

Add the egg and syrup and combine to form a firm dough. Turn the dough out on a surface lightly dusted with rice flour, roll out to a thickness of ¹/₄ inch and use animal cutters to cut out 20 cookies, rerolling the trimmings as necessary. Transfer the cookies to the prepared baking sheets.

Place in a preheated oven, 325°F, for about 10 minutes until golden. Remove from the oven, leave for a few minutes to harden, then transfer to a wire rack to cool.

Mix the confectioners' sugar with the boiling water and add the coloring, if using, then smooth over the biscuits or pipe icing details. Decorate with candies, if using, and allow to set.

For jeweled Christmas cookies, make the dough as above, then cut out shapes using Christmas cutters. Place the cookies on the prepared baking sheets and make an indentation (or more than one, if liked) in the dough, making sure you don't push all the way through. Roughly crush different colored hard candies and put a few pieces into each indentation. Cook as above and gently dust with confectioners' sugar once cooled.

lemon, pistachio, & fruit squares

Preparation time **10 minutes**, plus chilling
Cooking time **20 minutes**
Makes **15–20**

butter, for greasing
grated zest of 1 **lemon**
½ cup chopped **ready-to-eat dried dates**
¾ cup **unsalted pistachio nuts**, chopped
¾ cup **slivered almonds**, chopped
½ cup **light brown sugar**
1½ cups **millet flakes**
1¼ cups **gluten-free cornflakes**, lightly crushed
13 oz **can condensed milk**
3 tablespoons mixed **pumpkin and sunflower seeds**

Grease an 11 x 7 inch baking pan.

Mix together all the ingredients in a large bowl until well combined and spoon the mixture into the prepared pan.

Place in a preheated oven, 350°F, for 20 minutes.

Remove from the oven and allow to cool in the pan. Mark into 15–20 squares and chill until firm. Store in an airtight container and eat wthin 3–5 days.

For chocolate fruit & nut squares, place 3 oz gluten-free white chocolate and 3 oz gluten-free bittersweet chocolate in separate heatproof bowls over saucepans of simmering water and leave until melted. Drizzle over the cooked and cooled squares and allow to set.

bite-sized mince pies

Preparation time **10 minutes**,
plus chilling
Cooking time **15–20 minutes**
Makes **24**

1 cup **rice flour**
1/3 cup **butter**
2 tablespoons **superfine
sugar**
1/4 teaspoon **ground
cinnamon**
2 tablespoons **cornmeal**
grated zest of **1 orange**
1 **egg yolk**

Filling
1 1/2 cups **gluten-free
mincemeat**
1 tablespoon **brandy**
1/4 cup **slivered almonds**,
roughly chopped, plus extra
to decorate
1 oz **marzipan**, frozen and
then grated

Place the flour and butter in a food processor and whiz
until the mixture resembles fine bread crumbs or blend
by hand in a large bowl. Stir in the sugar, cinnamon,
cornmeal, and orange zest.

Add the egg yolk and enough cold water to mix to a
dough. Wrap in plastic wrap and chill for 30 minutes.

Roll out the pastry gently between 2 pieces of plastic
wrap to a thickness of 1/4 inch and use a 2 1/2 inch
cutter to cut out 24 rounds, rerolling the trimmings as
necessary. Use to line 2 x 12-cup mini-muffin pans, and
patch any gaps with pastry trimmings.

Mix together the filling ingredients in a bowl, spoon into
the pastry cases and crumble over any leftover pastry.
Place in a preheated oven, 350°F, for about 15–20
minutes until golden.

Remove from the oven and cool for a few minutes
in the pan. Sprinkle with slivered almonds, then serve
warm with a dusting of confectioners' sugar and some
brandy cream.

For creamy mince pies, beat together 2 tablespoons
cream cheese and 1 tablespoon brandy, then spoon a
little of this mixture into the tart shells before topping
with the mincemeat filling and pastry crumbs. Cook
as above.

index

acknowledgments

Executive Editor: Eleanor Maxfield
Editor: Joanne Wilson
Executive Art Editor: Juliette Norsworthy
Designer: Penny Stock
Photographer: William Shaw
Home economist: Sara Lewis
Americanizer: Nicole Foster
Props stylist: Liz Hippisley
Production Controller: Caroline Alberti

Special photography: © Octopus Publishing Group
Limited/William Shaw
Other photography: Fotolia/JJAVA 15; Octopus
Publishing Group/Emma Neish 2, 4, 151, 153, 155, 157,
159, 163, 169, 185, 187, 193, 197, 199, 201, 203, 205,
207, 211, 213, 215, 217, 219, 221, 223, 225, 227, 229,
231, 233; /Lis Parsons 16, 92, 143; /Craig Robertson
23, 33, 51, 53, 63, 119, 123, 129, 139, 141, 161, 165;
/William Shaw 14, 38, 166, 190, 208; /Ian Wallace 144.